Tongue-Tied

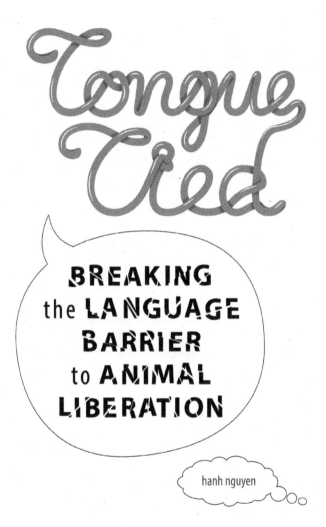

Tongue Tied

BREAKING the LANGUAGE BARRIER to ANIMAL LIBERATION

hanh nguyen

Lantern Books ● New York

A Division of Booklight Inc.

2019
Lantern Books
128 Second Place
Brooklyn, NY 11231
www.lanternbooks.com

Printed in the United States of America

Library of Congress Cataloging Publication information is available
upon request.

For Bubbles, Brandi, and Marshall

Contents

Prologue

L ANGUAGE FASCINATES ME. EARLY ON IN MY SCHOOLING, I BEGAN to show somewhat of a knack for learning new languages. I loved figuring out grammar rules and syntax—the almost mathematical patterns behind every word, phrase, and structure. I loved the logic embedded in language systems, and a lapse in an apparent pattern would frustrate my young mind to no end.

When I was a sophomore in college, I walked into *LING 110: Introduction to Linguistics* on the first day of class, having enrolled with the conviction of a self-proclaimed admirer of language and a grammar pedant who would obnoxiously fix others' grammatical mistakes. Little did I expect to gain a vastly more nuanced understanding of the many mosaic tiles that make up a language.

From phonology exercises to etymology lessons, I was blown away by all the ways in which linguistic origins tell us so much about cultural exchange and human history, like a moving record of societal progress over time. I learned the difference between descriptive and prescriptive linguistics, between trying to understand the complexity and patterns of a given dialect and blindly imposing foreign rules on it and pressing it into an existing mold. To this day, I regret not being a linguistics major. But fear not, dear reader—this is neither an esoteric discussion about the particularities of linguistics nor an ode to my fascination with the discipline. Carry on!

Linguist or not, you can't deny that language is important. Greek philosopher Diogenes wrote that although human beings are bound to other animals by virtue of having bones and sinews, reasoned thought displayable via language sets us apart from the so-called non-rational animals. (Substantive objections to his line of thinking aside, let's note for now only the importance Diogenes attributed to language.) Not just Diogenes, but many of us who haven't dedicated our lives to pondering the biggest questions that plague humanity would also argue that the ability to express meaningful language is a pillar of human intelligence. Yet for something that's so significant, something that's imbued with so much tradition and history, we give it little thought most of the time.

Language is a double-edged sword. It is one of the most beautiful aspects of human cultural heritage; at the same time, it's a weapon used to discriminate and dominate. Words can single-handedly set in motion a Shakespearean tragedy, alienate an entire section of the population, and even convince people that it's a good idea to go to war.

Non-standard dialects have often been reduced to being considered a mark of poor intelligence, a lack of education, and a dubious overall character. For instance, features of African American Vernacular English, the dialect spoken by many black Americans, such as "double negation" ("I don't see nothing"), have always been looked down upon and treated as something to be corrected by our education system. Yet they are governed by rules, and the double negative appears both in old forms of "standard" English (spoken by white people of European descent) and in contemporary languages other than English. The dialect is anything but random or the result of ignorance.

In that same year, as a sophomore in college, I was introduced to the animal rights movement after having already made the decision to adopt an ethical vegan way of living, prompted by a video very generically and unenticingly titled "Meat Video" (to this day I still wonder why I ever clicked the *play* button). I was exposed for the first time to ideas about social justice. It was only a matter of time before I circled back to my budding interest in linguistics; I slowly began to grasp the power of discourse in determining the success of social movements—how the different narratives we tell can move us closer to or further away from our goal of a more just society.

Countless movements have taken advantage of the power of language and narrative to propel their respective causes, especially since the "linguistic turn" in social theory toward the end of the twentieth century, when long overdue attention was turned to language as a central mechanism in structuring power relations, oppression, and exploitation—and as a malleable tool to be potentially abused by society's dominant group to banish or bolster certain ideologies and to maintain the status quo and social inequity. Claiming, or in many instances reclaiming, certain aspects of language is a major avenue of individual and collective empowerment, whether it's individual words and expressions historically used to deride and degrade or oppressive narratives. The recent #MeToo phenomenon is a compelling example of those who have been victimized doing just that—they reclaimed the first-person voice in narratives of sexual assault. Thus, my fascination with the different particularities of language evolved from vague intellectual interest to serious curiosity about how activists could use language to further bring to light ethical questions involving other-than-human animals that our culture habitually prevents us from asking.

Just as LGBTQ+ activists in the 1980s reclaimed the word "queer," originally used to ridicule men who acted effeminately, I look forward to the day when we humans are able to reclaim the word "animal," and along with it our own animality, when that term no longer carries any negative connotation or demeaning undertone.

I am lucky enough to have been able to witness the tremendous growth of the animal rights movement just within the last few years. However, I can't help but notice that the increase in the number of people who refuse to fund the exploitation of other-than-human animals doesn't necessarily mean that we are all working to reverse gross misconceptions and negative stereotypes associated with our fellow animals.

We're living in a time when, in order to be fashionable, one clothing brand after another is dropping fabrics made of other-than-human animals' skins and hair from its collection. In 2019, my peers and I don't know what it's like not to have vegan milks, meats, and cheeses available in mainstream grocery stores. Yet these signs of progress don't necessarily signal that we have a better understanding of other animals or that we can now see them as individuals. For the most part, we still view other animals as faceless collectives. In a vague sense, we understand that it's wrong to use other animals for our benefit, but beyond that our cultural attitudes toward them receive little attention.

This is understandable, perhaps even inevitable. Because of the sheer enormity of the industries that profit off of other-than-human animals' bodies and labor, we're constantly trying to wrap our heads around statistics amounting to billions and thousands of billions of individuals killed for their skins and fur or in experiments, as well as individuals wasting away in circuses, roadside zoos, and on racecourses. What we have are only estimates, probably low estimates at that: we don't actually know how many other-than-human individuals suffer and die, directly or indirectly, at the hands of humans every year.

The massive scale and magnitude of the suffering we cause other animals impair our ability to see that suffering as it is—in psychology, this is a phenomenon known as psychic numbing. Joseph Stalin is reputed to have said that the death of one person is a tragedy, but the death of one million is a statistic. When a single human who eats other animals robs on average two hundred lives each year just by eating (this rough estimate was recently updated to include sea-dwelling beings because we can't ignore their plight any longer), it's easy for the conversation about individual animals to be drowned out by the weight of their collective suffering.

I now focus much of my work on showing others, including those who consider themselves allies of other-than-human animals, how language, the very thing upon which our human pride hinges and which supposedly places us squarely outside of the animal kingdom, is used to justify our tyranny over the rest of animalkind and to perpetuate *speciesism*. Systematic oppression based on arbitrary species boundaries, as the word suggests, is no more legitimate than racism, sexism, or ableism— discrimination based on morally unmeaningful categories of race, sex, or physical and mental abilities. As an ideology, speciesism is upheld culturally, economically, and politically through its reproduction in not only linguistic patterns but also the myths on which society operates. Other-than-human animals are physically "tongue-tied" as they lack the vocal structures necessary to produce humanlike speech, though this doesn't equate to an inability to grasp the rules of human languages; they are also metaphorically and systematically silenced. They are denied personhood, agency, and political power. The language barrier that stands between us and other animals serves both as a practical communication lapse and to instill speciesist notions that bar us from recognizing other animals as complex individuals within complex communities, with languages and cultures of their own.

I have reoriented my endless picking-apart of grammar and diction toward a new purpose. Not too long ago, my biggest pet peeve would have been the misuse of "there," "their," and "they're"; "we're" and "were"; or "then" and "than." Now, the most glaring faux pas I believe one could commit is to refer to an other-than-human animal as "it," which I stubbornly correct every time, either out loud or in my head. But this is not mere pedantry. I hope the urgency of directing our attention to this largely unvisited niche in animal advocacy becomes clear in the course of this book.

You may have noticed that I use somewhat "unconventional" terms to refer to the collective most humans would simply label "animals": other-than-human animals, other-than-human individuals, nonhuman persons, and so on. I go to such pains to delineate these subcategories for the very simple reason that I do not see and treat "animals" and "humans" or "people" as being mutually exclusive. Other-than-human beings, in their infinite heterogeneity, are all unique persons, even if our legal system and our culture at large have barely begun to recognize them as such. Admittedly, even the terms I have settled upon in this book are inadequate in capturing and honoring this diversity, and in using them I have not moved completely away from a human-centric paradigm.

Equally begrudgingly, I use speciesist terms in some instances while denoting their inaccuracy with scare quotes, or preserve such usages in original quotes while marking them with [sic]. Sometimes, speciesist language may also be used ironically as a means of criticism; for instance, many "owners" do not perform their duties as guardians of the other-than-human animals in their custody, but view them as no more than property or "pets."

Those of us who advocate for other animals often place emphasis on aligning our actions with our moral values, but what is often forgotten is that words, too, have enormous power. And if language is a tool to express our vision for our collective evolution, if we are committed to true social equity, the very words we speak must show it. A lot has changed for other-than-human animals, especially within the last few decades, but the fundamental anthropocentrism in our language is still pervasive. The intricate ways in which language constantly reflects and shapes thought make it a crucial component of social change. Linguistic violence enables and correlates to physical violence toward other-than-human animals. Thus, our language needs liberating from speciesism just as the cages and slaughterhouses of the world need emptying.

That said, I have not written this book only for animal advocates or even those who don't consider themselves activists but still read up on issues involving other-than-human animals. I do not want to suggest that your journey to a better, truer understanding of other-than-human animals should or will be linear. If a text about speciesist language is your first introduction to the struggle for nonhuman rights, welcome! I hope that you will seek companion materials that explain all the ways in which other-than-human individuals are exploited for human benefit, if you have not already done so, for that knowledge would enrich the discussion into which this book delves. I have deliberately omitted some of those accounts of exploitation in favor of a more focused argument.

With that, I hope I can convince you in the following chapters that linguistic change is absolutely essential if we're to reconnect and recognize our commonality with the rest of animalkind—if we're to create a more just world for other-than-human animals. Even if phonology exercises don't sound that enticing to you, you might just be surprised!

Introduction

The "Other"

I AM WHAT THEY CALL A THIRD CULTURE KID (TCK). I DID MOST OF MY growing-up not in the culture that appears on my passport, nor in the ones in which I spent most of my transformative years, but in an amalgam of all of those—in a sense, my own world.

When I left my native Vietnam for neighboring Laos at twelve years old—rather unexpectedly, as my mother had made the bold decision to accept a new job and move to a foreign country, taking me with her—I didn't have any conception of a multicultural upbringing. All I knew was that, suddenly, I had gone from a public school with a strict uniform-only policy to a private international school that allowed an open dress code. Abruptly, I was in a new environment where I had to speak English all the time, a language I had not yet mastered. The experience of starting at a new school—so momentous and terrifying to me—was a habit for my new classmates, many of whom were children of diplomats. And Laos, although similar enough to the only country I had known to that point, was at the same time vastly different.

My memory of school life in Vietnam was that it had been, for the most part, pleasant, or perhaps I left before I was old enough to be truly critical of the Vietnamese public school system and the homogeneity that it imposes. But, breaking free from it, for the first time I became aware that the norms that governed school life were as transient as the new friends I was making, who were constantly moving because of their parents' jobs. For the first time, my twelve-year-old mind must have had some inkling that I could deliberately choose to deviate from what was normal, whereas before, I had never even questioned that normal. Rather than having an identity handed to me, I found I could shape my own; rather than automatically indulging in the feeling that I belonged, I had to work to construct a sense of belonging.

When I moved again in tenth grade, this time to Thailand, I made these discoveries all over again. Home is quite literally a feeling for TCKs. Even after many years of living in Thailand and doing volunteer work, I still feel oddly out of place every time I visit my parents in Bangkok. All I am is a visitor, brushing against that culture in the most superficial way.

My playing the role of an outsider is both real and imagined, and language no doubt plays a part. I often say, half-jokingly, that I have no mother tongue. I have studied English since I was six; it has been my dominant means of communication since I was twelve; Americans tell me they can't detect any accent and that they'd never be able to tell I'm not from the United States. Nonetheless, I still don't feel like I'm fluent. Even when I go back to Vietnam, my heart sinks whenever strangers remark that I speak Vietnamese with an "accent," the accent being not in my pronunciation but in the way that I construct sentences and carry a conversation—the subtler aspects of language intrinsically tied to a culture with which I've been so long out of touch.

Don't get me wrong—I'm fully aware that I speak from a position of incredible privilege. Despite having spent the first few years of my life in a country with a relatively troubled recent history and having parents who themselves lived through a major war, I was brought up within the new middle class in the country's capital, never knowing hardship or displacement. I never felt the need to contemplate my position in society—politically, socially, culturally. Being a TCK may have complicated the question, "So where are you from?" but in return I would develop an understanding of a crucial principle: that no one should feel out of place, even as an "outsider." My environments taught me to not only tolerate but indeed expect diversity and constant flux as a fact of life.

When I became an ethical vegan, and subsequently when I got involved in the animal rights movement in the United States, where I worked full-time for an animal rights organization, I was and am still guided by these fundamental values. My increasing involvement in this cause has always been a natural progression, not just because I have believed myself to be an "animal lover" since I was young, but also because other animals are physically rootless in a human-dominated world, just as I may be seen as culturally rootless (as my mother often says with exasperation). The fact that they are excluded from our moral community and silenced on every level—social, political, judicial—is an immeasurable injustice. Overlooked though it is, this injustice presents a threat to a sovereign and equitable social order.

This book is a combination of personal reflections based on my experience with different languages and cultures, as well as on findings from my research; it is also a written exploration of recurring themes in my work and activism. It represents a body of observations that I want to share with you, taken from my own life and gleaned from those who have studied and written about the subject for much longer than I have. It also embodies my own journey in learning to uncover my cultural and linguistic heritage in the context of my activism, to find a meaningful vocabulary to articulate my most deeply held convictions to my loved ones in a language that we all understand.

It is not meant to be a definitive guide but rather a conversation starter and habit-building tool. My hope is you don't take the suggestions made in this book at face value but instead question them, contribute to them, improve upon them. I hope you make a habit out of carefully considering the other-than-human subjects in your daily vernacular just as you should take a moment to consider how these individuals are affected by your consumption choices, so that one day all animals may be given truly equal consideration based not on their species but on the universal desire for life, liberty, and happiness.

Other Animals, According to Humans
A Very Brief History

O UR VIEW AND TREATMENT OF OTHER ANIMALS TODAY ARE INFORMED by a thick historical backdrop. With the objective in mind of understanding how our attitudes evolved over time, I look to the legacy we've inherited over thousands of years from different philosophical schools, religious texts, works of literary genius, folklore, and everyday wisdom gathered by humans of the past.

At the outset, I want to emphasize that this assessment is not meant to inspire any excuse for our present behavior based on an appeal to tradition, but rather to fully grasp the breadth and depth of the problem we are trying to tackle. To change the course of history, we must look back at what that history is.

The present chapter provides some context for the dissection of different chosen linguistic tropes that follows in this book—common usages extracted from my experience with two main cultural traditions, my home country (Vietnam) and the one in which this book was written (the United States). As such, my focus is on the Eurocentric or so-called Western canon, which I will explore alongside philosophies and folk religions originating from the East, namely those that continue to shape contemporary Vietnamese society.[1]

So, how did we come to view other animals as we do now?

Much of Western philosophical thought is indebted to Aristotle, known simply as "The Philosopher," and the "question of the animal" is no exception. Aristotle posited the ensouledness of all beings, giving both a taxonomy of souls (vegetative, sensitive, appetitive, locomotive, and intellective) as well as a hierarchy based on reason. Not only did he not place emphasis on a human–other animal divide, but he also actually admitted that the human is an animal—a rational animal, to be precise. In his view, all living beings are thus linked by virtue of having a soul, even if sharing a common animal nature is not enough to justify equal consideration, just as sharing a common human nature does not put natural slaves and masters on equal footing. (Aristotle's rather tautological definition for a natural slave was "anyone who, while being human, is by nature not his own but of someone else"—one whose "work is the use of the body, and . . . this is the best that can come from [him].") He concluded in *Politics*: "We may infer that, after the birth of animals, plants exist for their sake, and that the other animals exist for the sake of man."

The Ancient Greek adjective *alogon*, or "without *logos*"— without both rationality and language—was used to describe other-than-human animals; initially, it differentiated them from human soldiers in a military context. Based on its association with battle, as a noun, the word has also come to mean "horse" in modern Greek. These linked meanings make sense, of course, in light of the word's origin in a society that strongly correlated verbal mastery with social standing. In this world, other-than-human animals, who allegedly lacked altogether the capacity for language and hence reason, fell on the opposite extreme of the spectrum as the masters of persuasive speech; in between them were marginalized groups consisting of children, women, foreigners, the uneducated, and those with communicative disabilities.[2]

In this context, it's not hard to see why barbarians were regarded with so much contempt in the ancient world; the original use of the term "barbarian" referred to all non-Greek-speaking peoples, including Egyptians, Persians, Medes, and Phoenicians. The Greek word *barbaros* came about because the languages these peoples spoke sounded to Greeks like gibberish—"bar bar bar." One may be inclined to note how utterly ironic it is that today, "speaking Greek" often means uttering nonsense, babble, or gibberish.

Not only was there, according to the Philosopher himself, not a clear line separating humans from other animals, but also the body of literary works from ancient Greece and Rome illustrates that human and other animal lives were deeply intertwined. In story, myth, and real life, other animals held diverse roles and functions, as companions, entertainers, laborers for "agricultural" purposes, means of transportation, and "creatures embodying divine power or being sacrificed to the gods."[3]

Communication between humans and other animals was ubiquitous. Homer's epic poems are filled with not only animal similes, but also actual other-than-human animals as augurs, subjects of oracles, or symbols. In Book 8 of the *Iliad*, Zeus, the father of all gods, sends an eagle, his favorite and the "surest of omens among winged birds," to convey his will to an army of warriors. Homer's audience would have enjoyed these encounters with other-than-human animals through art as well as in naturalistic descriptions of them since, according to Johanna Leah Braff, they "appeal to the familiar and the commonplace, and yet they are veiled in mystery—the animal is at once comprehensible and unknowable." If their appearances in Greek mythology and fables are any indication, there was no shortage of human admiration for other animals' majesty, strength, and sexual prowess.[4]

Also evident in classical literature and the mythological tradition is the fact that fantasies of human–other animal love and erotic engagement were socially acceptable and of great interest. *De natura animalium*, a third-century Greek miscellany on other-than-human animals, recounts elaborate stories of love between a white elephant and his Indian trainer, a snake and a woman, a dolphin and a boy, and a goat and her guardian. Although physical consummation of inter-species love could be seen as problematic, this kind of love, when spiritual and unphysical, represents in the text a philosophical ideal.[5]

All this is not to imply that ancient civilizations lived in perfect harmony with all other animals. The Romans treated criminals and military captives as well as thousands of free-living ("wild") animals as non-citizens (those who were excluded from the moral sphere); that is to say with extreme cruelty, particularly as part of the games—bloody and fatal battles in Roman arenas. Around 550 C.E., famed Roman statesman Cassiodorus summed up the common view of contemporary Romans when he suggested, albeit somewhat dubiously, that the word *barbarus* ("barbarian") was made up of *barba* ("beard") and *rus* ("flat land"); barbarians, which was what the Romans considered the Huns, Franks, Vandals, Saxons, and Goths, did not live in cities but instead made their abodes in the fields "like wild animals."

Christianity brought into the Roman world the idea of the uniqueness of the human race, a core tenet that was singled out from the Jewish tradition. Human beings alone possess immortal souls, as is declared in the New Testament. With this came the distinctively Christian idea of the sanctity of all human life: "So out of the ground the Lord God formed every animal of the field and every bird of the air, and brought them to the man to see what he would call them; and whatever the man called every living creature, that was its [*sic*] name" (Genesis 2:19 NRSV). "For every species of beast and bird, of reptile and sea creature, can be tamed and has been tamed by the human species" (James 3:7 NRSV). The line separating humans from the rest of animalkind was starting to thicken.

Even so, early civilizations in the Western world had a comparatively more nuanced understanding of the animal world beyond the human sphere, in direct contrast to the modern absolute dualism of "human" versus "animal." In Genesis, there are "the fish of the sea," "the birds of the air," "the cattle," "the wild animals of the earth," *and* "every creeping thing [*sic*] that creeps" (Genesis 1:26 NRSV). Appreciation for the diversity of the animal kingdom persisted well into the Renaissance. In fact, the generic naming of "animal" hardly appears in historical documents written in English before at least the end of the sixteenth century; a list was often used to denote more than one subcategory of other-than-human animals rather than a single collective word.[6]

To quote the Bard himself in *Timon of Athens*: "We cannot live on grass, on berries, water, / As beasts and birdes and fishes" (IV. iii.427–28). "Beast," as is clear from this context, is not a synonym of the modern catch-all term "animal"; "beast" here means neither fishes nor fowls but a large, four-legged, land-inhabiting animal, usually one who's grouped under the term "livestock." These inventories denote a perception of the world that, while still anthropocentric, was vastly more inclusive than that of modern human society. In this universe, instead of the modern, pseudo-generic "animal," there were "beasts" and birds, fishes and reptiles, and humans. Although only two—at most three—actual nonhuman characters appear in Shakespeare's plays, the plethora of animal imagery reveals the extent to which the contemporary human psyche was preoccupied with other animals.

The Renaissance attitude toward other-than-human animals preserved from preceding eras a sense of kinship and mandatory stewardship. Although humans still represented the *summa* of divine creation, we were considered somewhat of an extraneous add-on to an already orderly world. That humans were supposed to be the epitome of all of animal creation wasn't always seen in a positive light, as is evident in this passage from Shakespeare's *Troilus and Cressida*: "This man, lady," says Alexander to Cressida of the anti-hero Ajax, "hath robbed many beasts of their particular additions. He is as valiant as the lion, churlish as the bear, slow as the elephant: a man into whom nature hath so crowded humours that his valour is crushed into folly, his folly sauced with discretion" (I.ii.22–25).[7]

Indeed, it was understood that humans could stand to learn a thing or two from our fellow animals. The following biblical passage portrays other-than-human animals as sentient beings, capable of not only communicating seamlessly with humans but also imparting wisdom:

> But ask the animals, and they will teach you;
>   the birds of the air, and they will tell you;
> ask the plants of the earth, and they will teach you;
>   and the fish of the sea will declare to you.
> Who among all these does not know
>   that the hand of the Lord has done this?
> In his hand is the life of every living thing [*sic*]
>   and the breath of every human being. (Job 12.7–10 NRSV)

In the Renaissance world, human and other-than-human lives were still very much interwoven. It was believed that the range of sympathies and antipathies in the rest of the animal world shed light on the scope of human emotions, an idea that those in Western nations would later vehemently protest, among them nineteenth-century ethologist C. Lloyd Morgan. Morgan's canon, a now widely endorsed rule in animal psychology, instructs us that other-than-human animals' behaviors should be explained only in terms of base instincts, never as the outcomes of higher, "humanlike" psychical faculties.

The human–animal binary in Western thought, built upon an underlying ethos of human exceptionalism, acquired its modern form thanks to the philosophy of René Descartes. It was also during this period that the word "animal" came into common usage to mean other-than-human animals. In light of the damning beliefs that were to be popularized by Descartes, the word now seems woefully ironic and a fundamental contradiction—despite their alleged lack of souls, other-than-human animals are collectively called a name that derives from *anima*, the Latin noun for "soul," "breath," or "spirit."

Descartes was an otherwise distinctively modern thinker who made invaluable contributions to philosophy and mathematics. But like his Christian supporters, he no doubt saw the usefulness of declaring that animals other than humans do not possess souls in defending the dominant theological worldview of the time. Since consciousness cannot arise from matter alone, Descartes claimed, the immortal soul, created by God, explains humans' consciousness. Other animals are, then, mere machines or automata, and their behavioral responses to environmental stimuli are, he added, the mere equivalent of the mechanistic programming of a clock. They actually experience neither pain nor pleasure.

The reduction of all other-than-human animals to a single category in direct contrast to humans, a development observable also in our language, was no doubt informed by the Enlightenment's scientific and technological progress, which explained the preoccupation with human intelligence and ingenuity.

Many Western philosophers and writers from Descartes onward have defended such a philosophical divide, even though they may simultaneously recognize that a number of other animals may be entitled to humane treatment (which in many cases then, as now, meant only the absence of overt torture). This attitude persisted even after Charles Darwin presented his theory of evolution in *On the Origin of Species*—the provocative idea that humans and other animals share a common ancestry and that our evolutionary paths, although divergent, are nonetheless governed by the exact same mechanisms. Darwin held that our common origins are expressed not only as similarities in outward expressions and behaviors between ourselves and other animals, but, as he subsequently argued in *The Descent of Man*, also as a universal capacity for love, joy, and happiness, as well as sadness, fear, and loneliness.

The implications of Darwin's conclusions were monumental. *The Descent of Man* tells us not only that "the senses and intuitions, the various emotions and faculties, such as love, memory, attention and curiosity, imitation, reason etc., of which man boasts" might be found in the "lower animals," but also that humans' *moral* sense can be linked to social behaviors in other animals' evolutionary history that led them to take pleasure in each other's company, feel sympathy for each other, and perform services of mutual assistance. Revolutionary though this publication was, it apparently did not question our hierarchical understanding of the animal world as consisting of "higher" and "lower" species, and even the humbling realization of the "unity of origin" of humans and our animal kin wasn't enough to demolish deeply entrenched speciesism. The most progressive intellectuals, including Darwin himself, stopped short of changing their minds when it came to exploiting other animals for human benefit.

T. H. Huxley, Darwin's greatest champion, revealed just how deeply entrenched this ideology is when he wrote: "[N]o one is more strongly convinced than I am of the vastness of the gulf between civilized man and the brutes; or is more certain that whether *from* them or not, he is assuredly not *of* them. . . . Our reverence for the nobility of manhood will not be lessened by the knowledge, that man is, in substance and in structure, one with the brutes; for, he alone possesses the marvelous endowment of intelligible and rational speech. . . ."[8]

🍂

How the West typically characterizes Eastern cultures' interactions and historical relationships with other animals in contrast to its own worldview presents, I believe, profound contradictions. On the one hand, Westerners of modern times, especially "animal lovers," tend to condemn and voice their collective revulsion at some East Asian cultures' consumption of the flesh of dogs and cats—species that in the West are decidedly off the dinner table. Such ongoing practices are often decried as "barbaric." On the other hand, reminiscent of the romanticized stock figure of the "noble savage" in Western literature—connected to nature, uncorrupted by civilization, and guided by an innate goodness—there is a certain idealization of Eastern theologies and philosophies that has persisted since colonial times.

Even now, I often observe many in the animal rights movement invoking principles of *ahimsa* (nonviolence), compassion toward all beings, and karmic retribution—important teachings in Hinduism, Buddhism, and other "transcendental" Eastern traditions—in their activism, implying that ancient wisdom in the form of these teachings ultimately anticipates and even prescribes ethical veganism.

In reality, other animals are portrayed in much more nuanced ways in Eastern schools of thought that don't always align perfectly with the principles of modern animal rights philosophy.

In Buddhism, interactions with other-than-human animals are important for the light they shed on broader Buddhist principles. In Mahāyāna Buddhism, practiced in countries influenced by Chinese culture, such as Korea and Vietnam, human and other-than-human animals are seen as closely related: both have "Buddha nature"; both may reincarnate as the other; and both may ultimately achieve perfect enlightenment. The prominent Mahāyāna Buddhist text *Laṅkāvatāra Sūtra* condemns the practice of eating the flesh of other animals in the strongest terms.

On the other hand, although the Pāli canon (in the Theravada Buddhist tradition) does not expressly command abstention from eating other animals, it is evidently ideal. The text also leaves no room for doubt with regards to the sentience of other animals:

> All living things [*sic*] fear being beaten with clubs.
> All living things [*sic*] fear being put to death.
> Putting oneself in the place of the other,
> Let no one kill nor cause another to kill. (*Dhammapada* 129)

As in Hinduism, karma is an important concept in Buddhism, although it is understood slightly differently. In Buddhist teachings, the notion of karma originally helped one recognize unfortunate outcomes as being the result of precise causal chains of events ultimately stemming from desire and their unjustified concept of their conscious self. The term has since entered the layperson's everyday vocabulary, used to express a general cautionary warning against bad intentions and deeds. Coupled with a fear of karmic retribution, the knowledge that other-than-human animals may very well be one's past family members reincarnated serves as a source of anxiety for many with this belief and a warning against unnecessarily abusing other animals, however they define "necessity."

Nevertheless, it's important to note that the doctrine of karma implies that human souls are reborn as other-than-human animals because of misdeeds in their lifetimes. Not only do other-than-human animals represent bad karma, but they are also, by design, unable to improve or reverse it, a detail that early Buddhists (though not the Buddha himself) used—and present-day Buddhists continue to use—to justify other animals' inferiority to human beings and to legitimize our exploitation of them. Further, to be reincarnated as humans is for other-than-human animals the only path to enlightenment. I know not a few Vietnamese people who earnestly believe this and do not see a contradiction between killing animals with their own hands and expressing their wishes for the dying individuals to be reborn as humans.

Compared to Buddhism, the teachings of Kongzi (known in the West as Confucius) pay much less direct attention to the treatment of other animals. In fact, other-than-human animals appeared to be absent altogether from Confucius's moral compass: "One cannot herd with birds and beasts. If I am not to be a man among other men, then what am I to be?" (*Analects* 18:6). However, Confucius's influential follower Mengzi (Mencius) did consider other animals:

> A virtuous man (*junzi*) is caring toward (*ai*) nonhuman animals (*wu*) but is not benevolent (*ren*) toward them; he is benevolent toward the people (*min*) but is not devoted to (*qin*) them. He is devoted to his parents but is merely benevolent toward the people; he is benevolent toward the people but is merely caring to nonhuman animals. (Mengzi 7A45)

While it's clearly stated that other animals should not be completely excluded from our moral sphere, it is also apparent that attitudes toward one's parents, fellow humans, and other animals are to be practiced as "love in differentiation" (*chadeng zhiai*), not only love in different degree.[9] And whereas later generations of Confucians developed Mencius's views to claim that humans form "one body" with all beings, with eighteenth-century Japanese Confucian scholar Kaibara Ekken going so far as to give explicit recommendations against the mistreatment of other animals as a component of one's duty to "serve Heaven," a feature of the Confucian tradition identifiable throughout history is its focus on the human sphere and human beings as the "highest" form of life.

This anthropocentrism means that it is perhaps precisely human beings' special place within the natural and moral order that commands any sort of "humane" attitude toward other animal species. Indeed, both the *Mencius* and the *Doctrine of the Mean*, two of the *Four Books* of Confucian philosophy, teach that "to be human is to be humane," that sensitivity to the suffering of other living beings is key to being fully human and "serving Heaven." Interestingly, the cardinal Confucian virtue, *jen*, a word best translated as "humane," also shares the same pronunciation and linguistic derivation as the word for "human being."[10]

Daoism, another prominent philosophical tradition based on the writings of the semi-legendary Laozi (Lao Tzu), similarly holds many principles that can be construed to be in agreement with, or even anticipating, animal rights, but yet does not rule the use of other animals as immoral. Daoist texts, like most ancient Chinese texts in which other-than-human individuals have a large presence, show great appreciation for species diversity; other animals are not one category but consist of "beasts," "birds," "insects," and "fishes," with the occasional mention of "dragons" and "snakes."

The *Zhuangzi*, an ancient anthology of stories that exemplify the ideal Daoist sage, famously recounts the titular Zhuangzi ("Master Zhuang") praising the free movement of a group of minnows: "Such is the happiness of fish." Upon being asked how he knows that the fishes are happy, Zhuangzi replies: "You aren't me, whence do you know that I don't know the fish are happy?" He adds: "You asked me the question already knowing that I knew." The implication is that by virtue of the basic similarities between humans and fishes, we can intuitively understand them.[11]

For Daoists, *Dao* or the Way is that which "abides in all things," "the final source and ground of the universe" that unites humans and other animals. The core principles of *ci* ("deep love" or "gentleness"), *jian* ("restraint" or "frugality"), and *bugan wei tianxia xian* ("not daring to be at the forefront of the world") teach Daoists to see the self as part of a whole and warn against excessive consumption as well as the killing of other animals not out of necessity.

Strikingly, on several occasions the *Zhuangzi* also refutes the idea that human interference with other animals' lives is always for the better. In the following passage, it describes the misery of other-than-human animals held in captivity compared to the freedom of their free-living counterparts:

> "[The] swamp pheasant has to walk ten paces for one peck and a hundred paces for one drink, but it [*sic*] doesn't want to be kept in a cage. Though you treat it [*sic*] like a king, its [*sic*] spirit won't be content."[12]

At the end of the day, humans are also creatures dependent upon and of the earth, inseparable from other animal species. Unfortunately, for Daoists, who recognize the importance of the natural food chain, this leads to the conclusion that it is acceptable for humans to consume the flesh of others. Despite its sense of wonder toward other animals, like Confucianism, Daoism doesn't question the morality of using them for religious sacrifice, medicine, and so on.

❀

Vietnamese spiritual and moral beliefs are heavily influenced by a unique mixture of these three religious traditions, called *Tam giáo* (The Three Teachings), which is also the source of much folk wisdom and many superstitions surrounding interactions with other animals. Though none of the three repertoires of ideas from the start envisioned perfectly equitable relations between humans and other animals, as we have seen, these schools of thought interacted with and borrowed from each other. In the end, there are either explicit or implied canonical teachings in each tradition that are consistent with a general concern for other animals and an aspiration to practice kindness toward them.

Other-than-human animals figure prominently in traditional Vietnamese folk beliefs, deep-rooted practices of ancestor worship, and mythological tales that inspired enduring cultural festivities and rites. Vietnam being a traditionally agrarian society, the Vietnamese people have always had an intimate understanding of natural entities and other animals, who then become objects of worship and idolatry—these are not only "powerful" animals such as tigers, elephants, and snakes, but also "tame," even domesticated animals such as toads, dogs, fishes, and storks, who are encountered on a daily basis.

The symbolic power of other-than-human animals in Vietnamese culture extends to the most basic task of telling time. Traditionally, Vietnamese people have used a system almost identical to the Chinese zodiac, consisting of twelve animals, who represent not only time from the year down to the hour of the day, but also the unique character traits of people based on their exact times of birth.

Other-than-human animals, oftentimes imparted with magical qualities, play an indispensable role in Vietnam's nation-building and creation myths. Every Vietnamese person knows the common saying "descendants of the dragon and the fairy," and the legend that traces the Vietnamese people's origins back to the one hundred offspring of Lạc Long Quân, the Dragon King of the Mighty Sea, and mountain fairy Âu Cơ.

As other legends go, King An Dương Vương could neither have built nor defended Cổ Loa Citadel, the first fortified citadel in the first independent capital of the unified *Âu Lạc* kingdom (now Vietnam), against foreign invaders if not for the help of a giant golden tortoise named Kim Quy (literally "Golden Tortoise"). In the fifteenth century, it was a similar golden tortoise, or perhaps the same Kim Quy, who approached King Lê Lợi during a boat ride to retrieve a magical sword, which had been lent him by the gods so he could free the land from Chinese rule and reclaim independence. The famous Hồ Hoàn Kiếm (literally "Lake of the Returned Sword") in Hà Nội got its name from this very legend, which endures in many a Hanoian's psyche.

Even so, the question of using other animals to accomplish the most basic tasks of everyday life has never really been much of a question in Vietnamese people's minds. Vietnam being a melting pot of religions, some scholars say that rather than rigidly following any particular religion, Vietnamese people have a utilitarian approach to understanding faith, adapting religious principles to directly serve their quotidian needs, even when practical concerns produce theological and philosophical inconsistencies. Thus, even though Vietnam's population has always been at the intersection of different theological and philosophical schools, many of which are quite compatible with a progressive animal ethic, and even though the Vietnamese people have a rich history of complex relations with many different animal species, one might find it less of a contradiction that they ultimately extend this utilitarian philosophy to the treatment of other-than-human beings.

It might be said, perhaps, that for the practical-minded Vietnamese people, it's especially true that concern for a given other-than-human species corresponds to its proximity and usefulness to humans. It is precisely this acute awareness of the practical function of each class of other-than-human animals, which clearly segregates those to be worshipped from those to be raised and worked as "livestock" and "poultry" or those to be kept as "pets," that underlies Vietnamese people's attitudes toward the rest of the animal kingdom and the "natural world."

Many Vietnamese are very clear about compartmentalizing their feelings toward different species of other-than-human animals, and indeed in many cases different members of the same species. I remember an exchange with a young cousin, in which I tried to point out the absurd logic of fawning over cats all the while eating other animals, the only difference being their species. I must clarify that I had been an activist in the United States for a while by this point, and was used to seeing the uneasiness of many a self-proclaimed "animal lover" following their realization that their "love for animals" is, in fact, strictly limited to only certain species.

Imagine the culture shock I felt when my cousin declared, without a shred of ambiguity, that "cats are pets, and other animals are food." Walking away from that conversation, I wondered if his partial feelings, even if only toward "pets," would endure into adulthood, or if, like many others, including his parents, he would later come to think of "pets" only as toys to humor and appease children.

Whereas the knowledge that "meat" comes from animals doesn't always come naturally to children in the West, no Vietnamese child has any illusions about this basic fact of life. The reality is that I can march into any fresh market in Hà Nội and pay for a chicken or a goose to be killed and turned into "meat" on the spot. If I get out early enough in the morning, I may run into rural residents on their motorbikes, with a pig's lifeless corpse strewn across the back seat, just in time to be sold at the morning market.

When I was in elementary school, two rabbits whom I had been given as "pets" (insofar as they were mine to keep in a cage and occasionally look at) were killed for a family meal when they had grown too big and continuing to care for them was inconvenient for the adults in the family.

The twofold lesson here is not only that killing other animals for their flesh is a normal part of life, but also that so-called pets and food animals are not impermeable categories, which rings particularly true in a place where dogs and cats are still eaten. Since the species distinction is no longer sufficient, arbitrary lines are further drawn between, say, dogs raised on meat farms and dogs stolen from their families, both to be violently killed for their flesh. It may be said that cultures that are more exposed to open animal slaughter may not need to maintain cognitive dissonance by way of denying or undervaluing the mental capabilities of "food" animals in the same way as in the West.[13] However, one way or another, cognitive rationalizations are constructed to relieve negative feelings associated with killing living, feeling beings.

☙

From Homer, Aristotle, and the Bible, to Shakespeare and other Renaissance authors, to modern Western thought from the Enlightenment onward, the thread of anthropocentrism is woven into almost every discussion about the physical and moral space occupied by other animals, with many of these discussions attempting to give various reasons for our supposed superiority to all other animal species and more broadly human civilization's superiority to nature. The culmination of all this wrestling with the "question of the animal" in the Western tradition seems to be the human–animal binary we encounter everywhere today, which represents arguably the most blatant display of human exceptionalism in the current ethical landscape.

Even though most humans in the global North now have a vague sense of concern for the welfare of (certain species of) other animals, in many ways the invention of the pseudo-generic "animal" in the Western vernacular and imagination presents a unique hurdle, one that prevents us from recognizing our interdependence and threatens to push other animals into oblivion, even as we have come to rely heavily on the luxuries furnished by their bodies and labor. We shove the diverse species of the animal kingdom into this abstract category of the "animal," just as we remove more and more from our everyday lives both "domesticated" animals, whom we banish to windowless farms and laboratories, and free-living animals, many of whom are considered annoyances and face extermination, although we're the ones encroaching on their homes in the first place.

The abhorrent conditions of intensive animal "agriculture" (which nowadays may be more accurately termed "agribusiness"), which is most advanced in the Global North, and the extent to which our everyday actions disregard other animals' lives, necessitate this invisibility. Both physically and rhetorically, we've thoroughly erased real animals and replaced them with the representations we've constructed.

Although this erasure of other-than-human animals is most prominent in industrialized economies, sadly, even traditionally agrarian cultures like my own are rapidly catching up, aided by trade policies aimed at the globalization of goods, including animal "products." As if that isn't alarming enough, rising economies have shown that innovation can be exercised in all the wrong ways: China is already running high-rise vertical industrial breeding farms of as many as eleven stories to cram more enslaved animals into an operation, even when the land doesn't allow it.[14]

I have an inkling that many Vietnamese of my generation and our parents' generation would reject the thought of such dystopian operations. They seem like the sort one sees on TV when the reporter covers events happening halfway across the globe, never "over here," so close to home. Despite growing up in a rapidly globalizing world, with Western brands and fast food at our fingertips, our generation still inherits from our parents an idealized mental image of family farms that raise animals as their only source of income, and who eat better and are better cared for than even the humans in the household. I know I certainly would still be under this illusion had I not been presented with overwhelming evidence to the contrary.

Conveniently, a culture of abstraction and mythmaking makes it possible for us to continue denying other animals' personhood, undermining their agency, and repressing their power to resist. It allows for speciesism to persist when this insidious ideology can no longer hide behind intellectual fallacies. This is the challenge we face today.

2

"It's Just an Animal"

How Language Takes Away Personhood

M OST AMERICANS LEARNED IN ELEMENTARY SCHOOL THAT A NOUN is a person, place, or thing.

Where do other animals fit in, then?

They are not places. And lest one is tempted to put them in the "person" category, which of course means only human persons, one is reminded that to do so would fundamentally contradict humans' self-aggrandizing view of our own species. So other animals remain a forgotten category; in reality, though they are not things in the same way the computer I'm using to type this sentence is a thing, most of them are treated not much better than inanimate objects. According to grammar guides, they are "somethings." We ought to say "The fox *that* jumps over the fence," not "*who*." After all, they are "*just* animals." In the world of law, many of the most vulnerable other-than-human animals aren't even "animals" at all: the U.S. Animal Welfare Act, the only federal law regulating the treatment of animals in experimentation, exhibition, transport, and by dealers, uses an absurd definition of "animals" that excludes birds, rats and mice bred for vivisection, horses not used for "research purposes," and a broad category of "other farm animals."

An exclusionary definition of personhood is foundational to Western philosophy. The last chapter already hinted at this aspect of the Aristotelian view of philosophical and political personhood: Aristotle placed so much emphasis on political participation in the determination of who is considered a citizen—a full-fledged member of human society—that he didn't even put all humans on equal footing. Those who lacked the cognitive capacity to participate in deliberative or judicial office, according to his judgment, were fit only to serve as natural slaves.

As a result, in Western thought, personhood and the moral consideration to which a person is entitled as sociopolitical constructs have traditionally been inextricably linked to related notions of free will or personal power, equality, liberty, and rights. Even though Aristotle's views on slavery would horrify most people today, the worldview that defines modern Western society is one in which the patriarchal *Man* (capital "M") wields the power to overcome nature and his proverbial inner "beast" at every turn to transcend the realm of mundane life in pursuit of happiness and spiritual enlightenment.

However much the idea of personhood might be proclaimed by philosophers to be universal, natural, or "God-given," in practice it's anything but. Time and again, personhood has served as a political tool to grant rights or revoke them at will, to reinforce the boundaries of civilization and exclude entire groups, human and otherwise.

In practice, those considered "subhuman" or "quasi-animal" beings have always conveniently occupied the buffer zone between civilized *Man* and the "brutes." Comparisons to animals or animal bodies undermine personhood so effectively because other-than-human animals can claim none to begin with.

In ancient China, peoples other than the Han Chinese were said to have characters that made them closer to animals. In fact, the word *Ti* (referring to northern barbarians) was written with the Chinese radical (a graphical component of a character) meaning "dog," while the word *Man* (referring to southern barbarians) was written with the radical meaning "worm."

Anti-Semitic propaganda disseminated under the Nazi regime in order to instill fear and disgust among the population frequently compared Jews to lice or rats who carried disease, flooded the continent, and devoured precious resources.

Leading up to the Rwandan genocide, which destroyed 800,000 members of the Tutsi ethnic group, radio messages and propaganda called Tutsis "cockroaches" who needed to be exterminated for the country to prosper.

In 2018, we seem as far as ever from a "post-racial America" as newspapers report on police officers calling black Americans, whether they are adults or just children, "wild animals" to be "put down."[1] Animalization has come to mean the same as the worst form of degradation—*dehumanization*.

Similarly, in Vietnamese, the word *súc sinh* is such an insult to one's dignity and humanity that it could form the basis of a lawsuit. *Súc* in Sino-Vietnamese means "to raise," while *sinh* refers to a living being. *Súc sinh*, which shares the same root as *súc vật* and *gia súc* (*gia* meaning "house" or "residence"), translates to "cattle" or "livestock"—species of animals raised for their flesh or for their labor who are thought to be by nature unintelligent and unclean, the most despised of all animals. By the same token, those deemed "barbarians" or "savages" are said to exhibit behaviors close to those of "wild" animals; they are often described by the words *thú tính* or *dã tính*. *Thú* here is the equivalent of "beast," while *dã* means "wild," and *tính* translates to "characteristics."

❦

Today, most English speakers still refer to most other-than-human animals by the same pronoun used to refer to a table—"it"—whereas many beloved vehicles, mechanical objects, even musical instruments are metaphorically gendered as "she" (they are seldom "he," this asymmetry often being attributed to the historical objectification of women), and these material possessions are given infinitely better care and more respect. An exception to this established custom is clarified in both the *Publication Manual of the American Psychological Association* (APA style) and *The Associated Press Stylebook* (AP style), which rule that an other-than-human animal with a name may be referred to using gendered pronouns. Only when the relationship is personal is it acceptable to use "he" or "she" when referring to that individual. A news article about a dog named Skippy may actually use "it" to refer conceptually to all dogs and specifically to Skippy before his name is mentioned—from then on, the pronoun "he" may be used.

There is hardly any species whose members are always either "he" and "she" or "it." Pronoun use tracks interpersonal relationships more so than species boundaries. That is, "s/he" pronouns are only extended to some of those who come into close contact with humans: other-than-human animals earn their gendered pronouns—and, by extension, their gendered identity—only through their association with humans.

Individual names are even rarer, largely restricted to those whom we really like and keep in our homes, who may be allowed to have an identity the way we do. Even then, the legitimacy of these names may not be fully recognized, and may even be diminished: some news articles still encase other-than-human subjects' given names in scare quotes, especially in the case of names that sound a little too "human." By contrast, a "stray" dog, a free-living wolf, and a pig farmed for their flesh are not important enough to us that we have names for them, so they all share the same objectifying pronoun. Now, it's interesting to note that many adult humans would also refer to infants as "it"; they are not proper subjects in the sense that they have not fully developed a personality or self-awareness. Human infants nonetheless still obviously enjoy the benefits of being human, as their perceived lack of personhood doesn't justify caging, beating, or otherwise mistreating them.

This is, in all likelihood, not a coincidence. Before 1847, when a case brought to the New York State Supreme Court on behalf of Mary Ellen, an abused ten-year-old girl, won a legal milestone for children's rights, children were in a very concrete sense the property of their parents, who could treat them however they deemed fit. A popular, if apocryphal, account of the court proceedings quotes Henry Bergh, founder of the American Society for the Prevention of Cruelty to Animals (ASPCA), who took it upon himself to help the child. Bergh reportedly said: "The child is an animal. If there is no justice for it as a human being, it shall at least have the rights of the cur in the street. It shall not be abused."[2] The statement may be fictional, but the sentiment is not.

Although there have been many victories for children's rights since then, children are in the same situation as other-than-human animals in that they are considered inferior beings and vulnerable members of society; their rights are recognized on a discretionary basis, if at all. Modern child-trafficking and the selling of children into slavery or forced marriage, sometimes by their own parents, begs the difficult question of whether we have truly progressed past our view of young humans as property, as "somethings" rather than "someones."

Similar human-centric distinctions in pronoun use exist in Vietnamese. A notable characteristic of the Vietnamese language is its intricate system of pronouns, which plays an important role

in "deference rituals" and in maintaining a strict social order.[3]
The pronouns used vary depending on one's age, attitude,
and the level of respect demonstrated toward the person being
addressed. Within this system, distinct third-person pronouns
are used to express respect for people who are older or those who
belong to a social class at least equal to one's own, such as *anh*
(referring to an older man), *chị* (referring to an older woman), or
the plural *họ*.

By contrast, *nó* (singular) or *chúng* and *chúng nó* (plural) are
third-person pronouns that one may use when "talking down" or
that imply the lower rank of the person being referred to. These
pronouns are used for other-than-human animals, children, or
lower classes of adults, including criminals, low-lifes, or villains
in a story. Although the Vietnamese pronoun system does not
completely reduce other animals to the status of inanimate objects
in the way that the English "it" does tacitly, there is a palpable
degree of condescension. Tellingly, *con* as a noun means "child"
or "small thing"; as a classifier, it indicates other-than-human
animals and various classes of objects; and it also functions as the
pronoun used in conversation with one's child or a person much
younger than oneself, the generic pronoun for other-than-human
subjects, and an infantilizing, if not outright condescending,
pronoun for women. On the rare occasion a human addresses an
other-than-human person directly—speaking to instead of about
them, the pronouns used are often *tao* (offensive "I") and *mày*
(offensive "you"), which often convey a derogatory undertone
or else indicate extremely informal language used only between
close friends.

Although the exact form that it takes varies between
languages (for example, in French, a gendered language, every
noun, including inanimate objects and other-than-human animal
species, is either masculine or feminine, and pronouns follow this
classification), the use of pronouns with regards to other-than-

human referents is in many ways symbolic of our glaring failure to recognize other animals as individuals.

Even so, there is no dearth of evidence of this attitude elsewhere in our vernacular. Take for instance the plural of "fish," which is still "fish." I believe it is no coincidence that many of the nouns with invariant plurals denote other-than-human animals—"deer," "elk," "antelope," "sheep," "fish," "cattle," "swine"; these are often species who have historically been either herded or hunted, especially for their flesh, as a theory in linguistics suggests (though it remains unproven). It has been suggested that the fact that "herd" animals are often grouped together as homogenous masses and the custom of referring to hunted animals in the singular ("We hunt bear, otter, beaver, deer, rabbit, raccoon, turkey . . .") may very well have helped inhibit plural regularization during the evolution of the English language.[4] Indeed, some of these nouns may have started out as singulars of mass. For instance, Daniel Defoe's Robinson Crusoe observes: "I frequently caught Fish enough, as much as I car'd to eat." As a general rule and for the remainder of this book, I pluralize uninflected plural nouns that are species names in the regular way, by adding –*s* or –*es*, to emphasize the personhood of each referent.

If the personhood of other-than-human mammals is already overlooked, the question of fishes' personhood must seem ludicrous to most of us. One need only look at how thoroughly fishing and industrial "aquaculture" have abused the ocean and the beings who call it home, or how their catch counts don't even attempt to provide an enumeration of the individuals caught, measuring them only by weight, in tons. And imagine, if you will, a mirror universe in which your biological classification stood in as a verb for another species' torture, mutilation, and murder of you and those of your kind, all in the name of a sport or a wholesome "outdoor" "father-and-son" activity. Isn't that precisely what "fishing" is? When they are quite literally "fished out" of their home, fishes have not merely been caught—they become "catch."

Indeed, except for the few animals whom we share our lives with, we humans think of most other animals as faceless masses, exemplified by the environmental protection movement's mission to protect "endangered species," even when individual members of that species are not themselves under immediate threat. It is also not the case that we distribute our concern for all endangered species evenly. The species that garner the most attention and appear most often on conservation organizations' posters are invariably those who have aesthetic value to us— so-called charismatic megafauna, such as polar bears, white rhinoceroses, pandas, and whales. It is largely the loss of aesthetic value implied by these species' extinction that we lament, not so much the fact that their disappearance may cause real suffering for other beings in the same ecosystem.

The language used to refer to free-living other-than-human animals makes it especially clear that we deal in "populations" and "species," catch-all terms and abstractions, of which individuals are merely lifeless "samples," "specimens," or "units." There are no interpersonal relationships between these identical units. The individual is already metaphorically dead, subsumed into the collective noun. One may receive a hefty fine for illegally poaching or trading an endangered species (that is to say, an individual or individuals belonging to said species), but the death of a "common" deer is no tragedy—indeed, it may even be construed as beneficial "population control."

At the other extreme, "invasive species" need to be mercilessly "culled." In December 2018, Congress passed a bill to allow sea lions in the Pacific Northwest to be persecuted for eating salmons to live, in order to protect the latter. (Curiously, no matter how much destruction we bring upon other animals and their homes, we humans never fall under this definition of "invasive," and our intrusiveness is instead branded as the price of progress.) Despite these radically different reactions and rationalizations, the price paid by each individual target of human violence is equally tragic.

Similarly, the other-than-human animals whom we purposely breed in order to exploit are so dispensable that for corporations they are reduced to ear-tag numbers; for consumers they are represented by product codes. Like all animal species subject to "selective breeding," "Thoroughbred" horses who are bred to be raced when they are mere teenagers are never their own persons existing in the now; of utmost importance is the purity of their blood—their membership of a lineage extending far into the past and the future. If they are genetic successes, they in turn become breeding "stock."

At the most fundamental level, we bundle together all other-than-human species and speak in the most generic terms of "animals," which twentieth-century French philosopher Jacques Derrida denounces as a violent gesture in itself: to do so is already to enclose "the animal" in a cage and flatten radical differences; it is a conceptual simplification with very real, violent consequences. Not only do we act as if humans don't fall under that classification (we habitually say "animals *and* humans" or "animals *or* humans"), but the very word "animal" by default carries with it connotations of inferiority. That we see other animals more as a type than as individualized identities is further exemplified by the idiom "a different animal," in which the generic naming of "animal" extends beyond the biological definition.

Even for animal advocates, being reminded daily of the enormity of the atrocities we are working to end means we may temporarily forget to look away from the statistics once in a while, even as we ask others to adopt a vegan lifestyle to spare up to two hundred lives per year—of whom X are cows and Y chickens and Z fishes. In my own research, I often have to stop and remind myself that each footnote, each entry in a database I come across, correlates with an individual with a face and a story.

❦

When you deliberately look past another's personhood, you only see them as a means to an end, as nothing more than an instrument. Some of the historical events that for us represent the most grievous affront to human rights demonstrate this principle. For instance, Korean girls and women who were forced into sexual slavery by the Japanese Imperial Army during World War II were called "comfort women."

Other animals' statuses in a world that has come to be dominated by humans are similarly decided by names that recognize them only for their designated function and coerced labor.

"Farm animals" and even the proposed alternative, "farmed animals," used by many animal advocates, obscure the ruthlessness of a system that operates under the guise of the benign concept of "agriculture," instead aligning its victims' forced participation with their identities or their lives' purposes; the inside of the "farm" is likely the only reality they will ever experience. "Pets" is, by definition, only a slight improvement upon "plaything," referring to other-than-human beings "tamed" and kept for pleasure. Likewise, "service animals" or "emotional support animals" and even "companion animals" identify beings by their potential benefit to humans. Although profound bonds are certainly forged between many humans and their "service" or "companion" animals, we as a society care only that these nonhuman others provide their companionship as a service to humans, and as such may fly with their caretakers under an airplane seat instead of as cargo. Other common examples, such as "hunting dogs" and "dairy cows," also come to mind.

Many of the other-than-human animals exploited by humans come to be defined by the place that confines them and the system that enslaves them; for example, "laboratory rats." The place of imprisonment sometimes stands in as the subject of a sentence to imply all of the individuals trapped inside that structure, as if they were the equivalent of machinery attached to the building ("Pullet barn likely a totally loss from fire"). Syntactically, the term "farm animals" is not different from "sea animals" or "land animals"— that these individuals "live on" the site of their exploitation almost seems like a matter of biological necessity. Likewise, we have adopted the industry term "zoo habitats," which makes glorified cages and prison cells seem homely, a perfectly adequate if not superior substitute for the natural homes of the zoo's "residents." In Vietnamese, the word for "rat" literally translates to "sewer mouse" (*chuột cống*), perpetuating stereotypes about the species as unclean and disease-bearing beings.

❦

In the same way their personhood is reduced to their function, other animals are seldom more than the sum of their parts. The human gaze is invariably a violent one, slicing other animals into "breast," "thigh," and "drumstick"; "loin," "ham," and "shank"— even while they're still alive. Other-than-human animals' flesh isn't just labeled by parts, but also by biochemical makeup as "animal protein" or particular types of "fats"; their flesh is broken down into cellular components so that it may be replicated or reproduced as an infinite resource. Diverse groups of sea-dwelling animals are rendered edible through their classification as "seafood" (the French go so far as to call them *fruits de mer*, literally "fruits of the sea"); their flesh, however, is not "meat."

After all, exploited other-than-human animals are not perceived as separate from the various "products" that can come from their bodies. Many humans are able to look at a "cute" picture of a chicken, or maybe even a real-life pig standing in front of them, and still utter words such as "tasty" or "breakfast" in reference to that other-than-human individual.

The process whereby the living being is reduced to lifeless cooked flesh is thoroughly truncated. Because they're not human, their once-moving body, now a lifeless "carcass" (which in itself is less dignified than a human "corpse"), magically becomes various cuts, or altogether undifferentiated "meat." Pigs become "pork," cows become "beef," and chickens become, well, "chicken." In the last example, the noun may stay the same, but "the *chicken*" on the plate no longer has any connection to "*the* chicken" whose life was extinguished for that meal.

We have "grass-fed beef" and "grass-fed dairy," but the cow who presumably eats the grass is out of the picture altogether. We have precisely measured and packaged Quarter Pounders. A chicken's wings, stripped of most of their functionality through domestication, become "chicken wings," which no longer carries any sign that a being once possessed or still possesses those body parts. The same principle applies to "mink fur," "goose down," "pig heart," and "cowhide" (which has amazingly even become one word!). In fact, the species names in these instances are functionally equivalent to adjectives. The other-than-human being as a subject no longer appears in the marketing of their body parts. An apparent exception to this observation, the term "cow's milk" keeps the possessive indicator, but now all cows exploited for their milk have been reduced to one generic being.

The "meat" and "leather" that we hack off other animals' bodies are made of the exact same stuff as our own skin and flesh. Likewise, there is little by way of real chemical distinction between "hair" and "fur," and yet to admit that this bifurcation separating hominids (some of the great apes such as humans, chimpanzees, and orangutans, and our fossil ancestors) and other animals is false would bring us dangerously close to the "lower beasts." Our lexicon reflects our diligence in enforcing these boundaries between human and other animal.

In Vietnamese, however, this linguistic dissonance is less pronounced. The word for "meat" (*thịt*) is the same for both human and other-than-human animal flesh. "Pork" translates quite literally to a compound word consisting of "flesh" and "pig" (*thịt lợn*); the same is true of chickens', cows', or any other animal's flesh. The names of many though not all body parts, such as "skin" (*da*), "fur" or "feathers" (*lông*), and organs such as "heart" (*tim*) or "liver" (*gan*), remain unchanged after the death of an other-than-human being. Again, these names apply to both humans or other animals, and perhaps most tellingly, there is an enduring belief in Vietnam that eating a given organ directly benefits the analogous organ in one's body, possibly due to the assumption of similar biochemical makeup. These divergences from the anglophone world do not mean that the belief in human superiority does not exist in Vietnamese culture, merely that it is rationalized and interacts with the language system differently.

Surprisingly enough, dogs' meat has historically gone by several names in Vietnamese, not all of which follow a plain and self-explanatory format, including *mộc tồn*—the two syllables are Sino-Vietnamese characters representing a play on a Vietnamese word for "dog." According to renowned historian Trần Quốc Vượng, the practice of eating dogs has its origins in traditional sacrificial rites; initially, only spirit priests and sorcerers consumed the sacrificed dog, and they did so only in private out of guilt. Euphemisms for "dogs' meat" emerged because of this cultural guilt, which predates the arrival of Western influence, a fact that may surprise many in the West.

Even when we do agree on which other-than-human animals to eat, we put different price tags on different body parts according to arbitrary, culturally determined taste preferences and (often misguided) beliefs about health. That Americans overwhelmingly prefer and are willing to pay a markup for white meat (chickens' breasts) still boggles my mind, as I recall many a family meal of my childhood in which I would be given the chicken's thigh, made up of darker meat, which was and still is considered the best part of the chicken's body. These market differences work extremely well with regards to the economic problem of surplus chickens' legs in the United States. We are no longer dealing with the dismembered bodies of chickens selectively bred to be obese and whose legs are atrophied from confinement by the time they are butchered, but merely minimizing the wastage that is a necessary part of production.

As raw materials, parts of the living other-than-human individual that might negatively affect productivity or even incur extraneous expense are systematically and methodically done away with. The mutilation of various body parts, which occurs mere days or weeks after the individual's birth, is reproduced syntactically through the plain language of "debeaking" and "dehorning."

Other animals' species and their species-specific features also become their defining, if not only, characteristic. We rarely refer to other-than-human animals by nouns other than their species name. By contrast, it would be quite odd if we only referred to each other as this, that, or somebody else's "human." Instead, we recognize each fellow member of our species as a unique "person," an "individual" whose experience isn't reduced to their humanness; because the point of reference for personhood is by default human, no qualifier to these terms is needed. We make use of relational nouns to introduce our partners, our friends, and our relatives, but often don't realize that other animals, including those we see only as "products," are also mothers, fathers, brothers, sisters, friends, peers, and leaders in their communities. All of them bring a "unified psychological presence," as the late philosopher Tom Regan puts it, to the world.[5] Language that is too literal a reminder of this reality can thus bring great discomfort. I recently stumbled across a photo online that showed a dead chicken's foot placed on top of an egg. Captioned "A mother's touch," the image elicited not a few comments on its dark nature. And even though a great number of other-than-human individuals are lifelong companions and best friends of humans, "my (dog or canine) companion" instead of just "my dog" would surely raise an eyebrow or two.

This paucity of relational words in reference to other-than-human animals oversimplifies their relationships—with humans as well as each other—and obscures categories beyond the level of species that encompass all of us and the shared experiences that connect us as animal kin.

But even more uncustomary is recognizing other-than-human individuals as proper victims. We dismiss the majority of them as merely "dumb beasts" ("dumb" being the Old English word for "mute, speechless") who have no concept of existence beyond immediate sensations of pain and pleasure, no moral compass, and thus no rightful claim to fair treatment.

They are not victims; they are neither enslaved nor murdered. Instead, they are "bred," "reared," then "slaughtered"—usually "humanely," of course, which makes us feel significantly better about the whole sorry affair. Worse, the euphemistic language developed by the same industries that physically morph living beings into profit-generating machines discursively turns the act of killing into "processing" or "harvesting."

No atrocity or massacre is ever committed against other-than-human animals. Most important, although trillions of other-than-human beings perish at the hands of humans every year, they have no entitlement to justice; in both word and deed, humans erase their suffering. Under an online news article about a fire that took the lives of more than 100,000 chickens at an industrial egg farm in 2016, a reader half-jokingly asked if there would be a barbecued chicken sale in the next few days to take advantage of the situation.[6] A news article covering a similar tragedy that left about 1,200 pigs dead notes that "no one was hurt in the blaze that caused more than $1M in damages."[7]

I once got into a heated argument with my mother over this exact issue—the use of the Vietnamese word for "victim" to refer to other-than-human individuals exploited by humans. The difficulty of my situation was compounded by the fact that the Vietnamese word itself (*nạn nhân*) by definition excludes other-than-human subjects. *Nạn nhân* is made up of two Sino-Vietnamese characters, one of which means "person," which is always understood to be human. The same character makes up the words *cá nhân* ("individual"), *nhân cách* ("humanity"), and *nhân đạo* ("humane," which is understood in the same context as in English). In the same vein, *người* in Vietnamese translates to both "human" (the species name) and "person."

As most humans have not expanded their moral circles to include nonhuman others, it's understandable that victimhood is still largely reserved as a human privilege. By questioning other animals' qualifications for victimhood, we relieve ourselves of the obligation to consider the ethics of our actions. The oft-cited reasons for which other-than-human animals are denied consideration as victims—that "they don't feel pain as humans do," that "they can't possibly know they are being mistreated"—sound all too familiar. If the general principle were true, that supposed reduced sensitivity to pain or inferior cognition rendered rights violations acceptable because of the victim's inability to recognize these as violations, why stop at other-than-human animals? We used to justify the atrocities humans committed against each other by reasoning that certain groups were less intelligent and less susceptible to pain by virtue of their physiognomy, skin color, or ways of life—views that were all supposedly backed by scientific consensus.

❦

Indeed, the low social standing we force upon other animals often is attributed to intelligence—or, in this case, a presumed lack thereof. As we consider ourselves the apex of evolution, we declare human intelligence the model for all living creatures to emulate. By this narrowly defined criterion, only a handful of species are smart enough to warrant our protection.

As far as most of us are concerned, a "likeness-to-human" meter continues to determine "evolvedness" and whether an other-than-human species merits consideration, again usually only to not be grossly mistreated. This standard is dubious at best, coming from a species that hasn't been able to agree upon a universal definition of intelligence for itself and has yet to learn to treat members of its own kind with perceived impaired cognitive function with universal respect. Intelligence, in itself a value-neutral aspect of a being's psyche, has throughout history upheld oppressive ideologies and, in turn, oppressive policies in areas such as housing, education, employment, and health care.

In the early 1900s, scientists were using the newly established IQ test to sort people with mental disabilities into different grades of deficiency based on their respective "scientifically quantified" mental age. These individuals, who were forced to bear such scientifically precise labels as "imbeciles," "idiots," and "morons," were also said to display "animal propensities" and "primitive savagery." Intelligence also figured prominently in the determination of racial demarcations.[8] In the early twentieth century, various immigrant populations from southern and eastern Europe, including Russians, Poles, Italians, and Jews, were called different "races," even though now they would all be categorized as Caucasian or white. They were considered to possess unstable personalities and inferior intelligence, which made them more suited to backbreaking manual labor and which threatened the advancement of American society as a whole.

By the end of the century, the category of whiteness had been extended to include the descendants of those who migrated from Europe decades earlier. However, the 1994 publication of the book *The Bell Curve*, which sought to prove the existence of a persistent black–white IQ gap, made it clear that a racialized view of intelligence remained as popular as ever and that we were far from overcoming our obsession with quantifying intelligence using only the socially dominant, Western conception of the term.

We now know that standardized tests of intelligence, including the IQ test, have failed miserably at capturing diversity in cognitive abilities among populations. They have proven to be plagued with cultural bias, are highly dependent on factors such as social, cultural, and economic contexts, and are not necessarily indicative of biological discrepancies. If anything, they perfectly illustrate disparities in education or employment opportunities and other measures of social inclusion. Just as modern scientific discoveries, notably the famous Human Genome Project, have shown that there is vastly more variation within a single population than across different populations of humans, thus discrediting the pseudo-scientific backing for arbitrary biological categories of race, scientists continue to uncover qualities and capabilities possessed by other animals that were previously thought to be exclusively human, a result that should have become apparent to all those who came after Darwin.

Studies published between 2015 and 2017 as part of the Someone Project showed that chickens and pigs have complex social lives and demonstrate empathy toward their peers; they also boast an understanding of numerical quantities and a symbolic language (one devised by humans, of course, as all animals speak their own languages).[9,10] And if there is still any doubt that other animals are capable of moral reasoning, studies at the University of Chicago have shown that rats will forego a chocolate treat to save companions in distress—say, being trapped in a pool of water, which made the latter very uncomfortable even if they weren't at risk of drowning—especially if the rats facing the moral dilemma have had similar unpleasant experiences themselves.[11]

As it turns out, how cognitively complex someone is has nothing to do with how much they resemble us or how fond we are of them. In fact, according to *Animal Behavior*, other-than-human animals who are cleverer according to our own litmus test have a higher chance of butting heads with and outsmarting us, thus becoming "nuisances" in our lives. Think of crows who make use of their excellent memory to steal food from us, elephants who figure out how to unplug the power source of an electric fence, and raccoons who quickly learn how to open specialized trash containers. Yet we label the same amazing individuals "pests."

These flimsy foundations upon which speciesism is built, no matter under what name—intelligence, reason, or rationality—all crumble upon close examination. We begin to realize how little we know about other animals yet how often we disregard them based on pure ignorance or otherwise biased assumptions.

One of the most arrogant proclamations that we humans have made about ourselves is that only our species is capable of language. We're always trying to teach this supposedly one-of-a-kind communication system to other animals. The late Koko the gorilla could comprehend two thousand words of spoken English, using a modified form of American Sign Language to express happiness, sadness, love, grief, and embarrassment. Alex the African grey parrot could say 150 English words and combine words to create new meanings; his last words to his human guardian reportedly were, "You be good; see you tomorrow; I love you." Bruno the chimpanzee, who was also competent in American Sign Language, used the very language of his captors to express KEY and CUT, demanding his freedom from the laboratory cage.[12]

Yet we have seldom taken the time to decode an octopus's color-shifting display or a whale's song. At the very least, the very canine companions with whom we share our homes for a decade or longer diligently learn many words in our vernacular, yet we seldom return the gesture.

Intelligence, especially when commonly and broadly understood to mean any sort of deliberate mental work as opposed to instinct, varies not only in degree but also in kind and dimension. Within our own species, we can identify social, emotional, logical, musical, spatial, and many other types of intelligence. Measuring other animals' intelligence against our own, which is what we've always done, gives a skewed and at best incomplete view of their inner worlds, the full complexity of which humans may never grasp. Mark Twain once said: "It is just like man's vanity and impertinence to call an animal dumb because it is dumb to his dull perceptions."

The mere fact that homing pigeons navigate by following human-made roads so rigidly that they sometimes fly around roundabouts before choosing the exit that would lead them to their destinations should be sufficient to show that the duality of "advanced" human intelligence versus "base" animal instinct is delusional, and our fixation on a singular metric of intelligence woefully misguided.[13] So when we rely upon a rhetoric that paints pigs as being "as smart as a human toddler," even as an argument for the ethical treatment of pigs and other animals, we inadvertently perpetuate this human arrogance and the notion that other-than-human animals are comparable to mentally underdeveloped human beings.

Much of this discussion also overlooks the possibility that "higher" (read: more "humanlike") modes of intelligence are not prerequisites for the experience of and ability to form values and preferences about the world. Thousands of years of social oppression have erroneously conflated our understanding of advanced reasoning capacity with conscious selfhood in our fellow humans as well as other animals. But you don't have to be smart "like a human" to be able to experience both the outside world and the state of being you.

In 2012, a group of prominent scientists, witnessed by Stephen Hawking, signed the Cambridge Declaration on Consciousness, confirming that there is no longer doubt that "all mammals and birds, and many other creatures" possess the neurological substrates necessary for consciousness.

Our understanding of not just "basic" or primary consciousness but self-consciousness of an order that constitutes personhood (as it presumably applies only to humans) is ever-evolving. Ironically, modern scientists are beginning to realize that a picture of human self-consciousness, or what our forebears would characterize as the human soul, cannot omit the physical body and our "animal nature," the very antithesis of our self-definition. Experience of the conscious self is experience of a self with a body, whose functions must be constantly controlled and regulated to be compatible with one's survival. Selfhood may very well be grounded in the biological mechanisms that we share with other living beings.[14]

Is there any good reason, then, to believe that other animals aren't self-aware, or that theirs is a "lower" consciousness? An absence of evidence, in almost all instances due to human error and oversight, must not be taken for evidence of absence. Unsurprisingly, we arrive at the conclusion that we are, in a sense, all beast machines, undoubtedly much to Descartes' chagrin if he were present to witness this exciting development in scientific discovery. We are all creatures of flesh and blood who act upon the basic drive to stay alive—a characteristic that differentiates animals, human and otherwise, from even the smartest of computers and artificial intelligence. That is what should hold moral weight, not the ability to exercise obscure political rights or pledge allegiance to any given society.

Repeated denial of other-than-human personhood and the subjectivity with which other-than-human animals experience the world and their conscious selves excuses us from facing the question of our moral responsibilities to them. This evasion also explains why the status of the legal person (and personhood in the legal context is in many ways weaker than the popular understanding of the term) has been granted to the Ganges river in India and the Whanganui river in New Zealand Aotearoa, and some constitutions now give nature broad rights,[15] when the overwhelming majority of other-than-human animals are still awaiting their turn. This means that humans in different cultures have already started to stretch the boundaries of personhood, even when this contract may be non-reciprocal: rivers aren't capable of moral behavior, least of all toward humans, nor can they fulfill legal and political responsibilities. (Readers may note the parallel to the *reductio ad absurdum* argument against legal personhood for other-than-human animals that hinges upon their inability to vote.) Nonetheless, we recognize that the significance certain environmental entities hold in various human populations' livelihoods grants them a place in moral discussions.

Through language, ways of experiencing the world that are incongruous with the human experience are further invalidated and belittled. We deny the existence of entire realities and repress the very being of the other-than-human victims of human supremacy, such that they are no longer thought of as subjects, singular and irreducible to insensate machines. Like other instruments of social control, language helps to legitimize and cement categories of "human" and "animal" as meaningfully separate from each other, *despite* the lack of any biological basis for such a division.

As the complexity of other animals continues to surprise us, as we slowly begin to learn that human consciousness is but one of a vast number of possible selves, it's time to acknowledge that other animals experience life in sometimes vastly different but equally valid ways; that their ways of knowing and being mentally active are not precursors but parallels to our own, and don't make any of them more or less of a person.

3

"Animal Instinct"

How Language Takes Away Agency

Open any textbook on animal behavior, turn on any nature documentary, and you'll likely run into the phrase "survive and reproduce." *Survival and reproduction are the fundamental driving forces behind all life*, it'll most likely read. It's common knowledge that animals (those other than humans, at the very least) act according to a singular drive to increase the probability of either, or both, and not much else. Everything that we observe them do can be conveniently attributed to basic instincts governed by this preconceived principle, which determines from the start aspects of other animals' behaviors that we choose to notice and study.

Descriptions of the same exact behavior, such as sleeping with another in close proximity, or "co-sleeping," are, in humans, laden with emotive effect, but void of any such language when it comes to other animals. Although different academic definitions of the term may vary, "co-sleeping" (further subdivided into room-sharing or bed-sharing) is consistently studied exclusively in the human context, chiefly between mothers and babies. A human mother may want to sleep in close proximity to her newborn to nurture the mother–infant bond, but only as a conscious decision, after having considered all the medical risks involved and warnings by healthcare professionals, and only when it fits into the parents' work schedule and nighttime leisure.

By contrast, other-than-human species, particularly free-living "pack" animals and "prey" or "herd" animals—those often disdained for their meekness—naturally sleep together in groups for mutual protection because the ubiquitous dangers in their environment necessitate it. Whereas co-sleeping (in humans) may constitute an "important bonding experience," as proponents of bed-sharing argue, rationalizations for social sleep in other animals are more likely to follow this format: *By staying in a group, the equids protect female zebras from potentially cuckolding males who may stumble across the herd.*

Despite the intimacy that nighttime togetherness brings, mothers in Western society are now strongly urged to reject their instinct to co-sleep for the safety of their newborns. Our eagerness to distinguish even the most primal of our behaviors, such as sleeping, from those of other animals underlies this aspect of social control—the deliberate privileging of one particular style of sleep, which has historically reinforced race and class divisions. In fact, up until the Industrial Revolution, social sleep was the norm in Europe. But since separate sleeping arrangements became commonplace in more industrialized economies, the now stigmatized practice of sharing sleeping quarters, still commonly seen in non-Western societies and historically marginalized non-white populations, stands in stark contrast to the Eurocentric private sphere, the hallmark of "civilization." Many now consider bed-sharing to be improper and even dangerous, and they may take as evidence for this view reports that purportedly link the highest incidences of infant suffocation during sleep, or Sudden Infant Death Syndrome (SIDS), to racial groups whose ancestry treats co-sleeping as normal.

According to Benjamin Reiss, in a 2017 article titled "Why do we make children sleep alone?": "Ensuring privacy at night was not just a health concern; it was also a matter of defining proper 'whiteness' or 'Europeanness.' While reformers endorsed solitary sleep as healthful and moral, they noted that 'savages' slept collectively—and this practice was somehow to blame for underdevelopment of the non-Western world." The article goes on: "According to the physician William Whitty Hall, author of a popular 19th century sleep hygiene book, individuals in co-sleeping societies were like 'wolves, hogs and vermin' who 'huddle together,' whereas in the civilized West, 'each child, as it grows up, has a separate apartment.'"[1]

In his autobiography *Fifty Years of Slavery* (1863), Francis Fedric writes: "Slaves live in huts made of logs of wood covered with wood, the men and women sleeping indiscriminately together in the same room.... This mode of living is no doubt adopted for the express purpose of brutalizing the slaves as much as possible, and making the utmost difference between them and the white man."

More broadly, the same maternal behavior is termed "motherly love" in humans, but "reproductive instinct" in mothers who happen to belong to other species. In 2013, a news article surfaced of residents living near a dairy farm in Massachusetts reporting "inhuman" noises "at all hours of the day and night," which turned out to be the cries of mother cows calling out for their stolen babies (newborn calves, being inconvenient byproducts of the industry, have to be taken away shortly after birth to reserve their mothers' milk for human consumption). These mothers were grieving the loss of their children. The police reassured the concerned neighbors, however, that the cows were not in distress and that the noises were a normal part of farming practices—a yearly occurrence.[2]

An explanation that some give in trying to undermine the disturbing reality that produces these heartbreaking cries is that mother cows are simply reacting to the pain in their teats after giving birth. Such rationalizations, of course, relieve us of our guilt and discomfort in recognizing that we are tearing families apart for mere profit and our own momentary pleasure in consuming the milk that is meant to nourish baby calves, and that the destruction of families and social ties has always been an essential tool of oppressors.

For us humans, who have come to thoroughly master and control the reproductive systems of domesticated other-than-human animals for our benefit, there is nothing mysterious about the "reproductive instinct" that drives "dairy cows" and "breeding sows" to "gestate" and "lactate." The "gestation crate," or "farrowing stall," is narrow, with slats in the flooring to allow urine and feces to fall through; mother pigs have barely enough space to stand and lie down in, and must always face in one direction. When the mother pig gives birth, she nurses through the metal bars of her glorified prison cell, which is supposed to "[prevent] her from unknowingly laying on her piglets." To say she "gives birth" is perhaps too generous: other-than-human mothers merely produce another piece of movable property—they "farrow," "calf," or "foal." The mass breeding of "Thoroughbred" horses for racing has become so efficient that mares are said to be "covered" by stallions; they effectively act as vessels for deposited sperm. A Thoroughbred foal is marketed at auction as "out of" their mother and "by" their father. Famous stallions in the industry father thousands of children in their lifetimes.

The bond between mothers and babies, as it threatens profit, is something to be worked around, even prevented altogether, as is the case on dairy farms. In the case of "beef calves," who may be allowed to stay with their mothers for longer, to artificially wean calves from their mothers' milk, spiked rings are inserted in the calves' noses so their own mothers won't let them suckle.

"Gestate" and "lactate" are terms that, save for medical professionals or biologists, no English-speaking layperson would use about an expectant or post-partum mother. Similarly, in Vietnam, it is often only rural folks, those often perceived as uneducated and boorish, who commonly use a crass word such as *chửa* to refer to both nonhuman and human pregnancies in the place of more cultured synonyms such as *mang thai*, used largely for humans. The inability to discern and uphold the fine distinctions between the two vocabularies meant to describe human or other animal reproductive behavior can oftentimes reflect negatively on a speaker and point to their low level of education and social status.

Elsewhere, the reproductive lives of other-than-human animals are similarly restricted to the sterile language of strict biology: mating and siring, cubs and broods. Matings can be planned, and "breeders" can choose to "cross" individuals with different phenotypes to select for the best characteristics to "improve the stock." This always implies domination and violence: painful "lip twitches" are used to restrain female horses, and stands or chute-like devices immobilize female dogs and cows as they are "mounted" (as in dog-breeding) or "artificially inseminated" (as in the dairy industry).

Today, even as we can look back on the great strides (human) women have made in our ongoing battle to reclaim ownership of our reproductive lives, the general belief that "maternal instincts" are internalized by female members of the animal kingdom, human and otherwise, continues to deepen the trenches of both sexism and speciesism. In the same way that some still regard human mothers as no more than "hosts" for human babies,[3] other-than-human mothers are verbally and physically reduced to makers of live capital.

In *And a Deer's Ear, Eagle's Song and Bear's Grace*, Theresa Corrigan speaks of the "tremendous variation in the mothering capabilities and interests of animals with whom [she had] lived." To illustrate that mothering is a reasoned choice and that those who are particularly interested in parenting don't discriminate between biological and adopted children, she tells a wonderful story of her friend Ted, a spayed Maltese poodle who "loves babies of any sort, kittens will do, ducklings are fine. . . . [M]othering, as many feminists recognize, is more than physically birthing. Spaying Ted did not deprive her of the maternal experience."[4]

In truth, "motherly instincts" are not experienced universally across species, nor is heavy involvement in parental care an exclusive characteristic of the female sphere in the majority of animals. Tremendous variation in parenting abilities exists even within species whose evolutionary histories favor parental investment (as we humans are well aware). The stress induced by living in captivity sometimes exacerbates negligent and even abusive parenting behavior. Moreover, assuming that other-than-human animals' are acting on mere instincts—that they inevitably want to have children once they reach sexual maturity—makes them inviolable, so we can force them to mate with partners of our choosing. In "breeding" other animals, we no doubt impose motherhood upon some who clearly do not wish or aren't necessarily equipped to care for biological children.

This biological essentialism extends to how we clearly categorize other species as "predator" and "prey": a binary of beings who are at the mercy of nature, caught in an eternal evolutionary tug-of-war. Without humanlike resourcefulness and inventiveness, they are unable to act outside their "animal instinct." By the same token, human "predators" are socially deviant criminals, made distinct from law-abiding members of society by their inability to control the "animalistic" urge to pursue their "prey." By comparing these humans to other-than-human beings who hunt by necessity, or labeling cross-species sexual violence as "bestiality" (indulgence in "bestial instincts"), we simultaneously underestimate the human planning that leads to such criminal acts and perpetuate the narrative that "animal sexuality" is in direct opposition to rationality.

To speak of other animals' emotional and mental realities is to run the risk of being accused of anthropomorphism. Indeed, having complex abilities and qualities doesn't make an other-than-human individual more interesting in their own right, merely more "humanlike." Technically speaking, however, "anthropomorphism" is the assigning of exclusively human traits to those who don't have those capabilities. As early as 1871, when he published *The Descent of Man*, Darwin told us: "[T]he first foundation or origin of the moral sense lies in the social instincts, including sympathy; and these instincts no doubt were primarily gained, as in the case of the lower animals, through natural selection." Darwin explained that even behaviors in humans that are puzzling at first can be attributed to the evolutionary race for reproductive fitness. Even without subscribing to biological reductionism, we would still have to accept that as much as we'd like to believe in their existence, scientific evidence is constantly blurring the supposedly neat lines separating us from other animals and disproving a view of human specialness.

We humans often pride ourselves on having opted out of the autopilot program that is set for "survival and reproduction." Yet when it's convenient, the appeal to our nature as animals can be easily whipped up to support an argument. We live in a patriarchal system that perpetuates toxic hegemonic masculinity, in which some men on the one hand can use the (male, mostly white) intellect as an indicator of their superiority as a sex, but in the same breath reason that humans' evolutionary history obliges women to retain rigid traditional gender roles.

We avoid difficult conversations that address problematic male behavior by saying "boys will be boys"; similarly, there's no need to discuss the moral implications of using other-than-human animals because, after all, we're meant to kill and dominate them. As evidence for this assertion, it suffices to point to our "canines," "big brains," or supposed position at the "top of the food chain." The logic of many a sci-fi horror scenario or thought experiment, where humans are subjugated by a more intelligent race, could be justified using the same thought process.

When our overreaching impact on other beings and their homes nonetheless raises the uncomfortable question of our ethical obligations to our animal kin, we turn at once to the laws of nature that supposedly govern the behaviors of all of the animal kingdom as a way out of all such moral dilemmas, at the same time that we decry the unfairness resulting from being special—that we and we alone have to carry all of the moral burden of our actions when other animals seem to be exempt from it.

*

There was a time when humans could deny outright that other animals could feel any emotion at all. Now that we recognize that position as being so clearly mistaken, the argument has shifted. We may share the same feelings and emotions, runs the reasoning, but experience them with far more intensity, subjectivity, and intentionality. In a conversation about the moral status of other-than-human animals, sooner or later someone is bound to cite studies purportedly showing that plants also feel pain and other rudimentary "feelings"; the *reductio ad absurdum* undermines other-than-human animals' claim to moral consideration.

Stories such as this, without fail, come as a shock to most humans: in 2011, a U.K. *Daily Mail* article reported a story about a mother bear on a bear bile farm in China, who strangled her cub before running head first into a wall, killing herself, saving them both from a life of torture.

Bile farming (harvesting a digestive juice through a permanent hole in the abdomen and gall bladder of Asiatic black bears for human medicine) often "leads bears [to try to] kill themselves." The article continues: "[T]he mother bear broke out of *its* [*sic*] cage when *it* [*sic*] heard *her* cub in distress . . . rushed to its cub and hugged it until *it* [*sic*] eventually strangled it before . . . killing *itself* [*sic*]" (emphasis added). The mother is "it," of course, because to grant her the correct pronoun would make her—and her motives— too eerily human, and the reader might too readily sympathize with an other-than-human animal who, as humans sometimes do when faced with ugly choices, defied biology and showed that she valued freedom more than life itself. As the pronoun confusion indicates, even the writer of this article struggled to completely overlook the courage and intentionality in this act of immense sacrifice.[5]

This story, along with anecdotes of bears safeguarding human children who were lost in the woods for days on end, directly challenges what fairytales have been telling us—that children who wander off alone are sure to be accosted and eaten by bears and wolves, and that vulnerable children in particular should beware of "wild" animals.

As a society and especially in our legal system, we are pretty comfortable deciding what a human's motive is for a given action, sometimes quite arbitrarily and without the person's input. Based on this perceived motive, they are either rewarded or punished accordingly. Most of the time, the person is given the benefit of the doubt. No matter how well documented selfless or altruistic behaviors (or, as in the preceding example, acts of parental sacrifice) are among other animals, their motives usually remain in question. True altruism in animals other than humans wouldn't make much evolutionary or biological sense.

When dogs, whom we call our best friends, save humans, it's because they have been trained to do so. If dolphins guide fishermen's boats out of the way of a storm's path, it's only with the expectation of a generous reward. When, in 1996, Binti-Jua, a female gorilla at the Brookfield Zoo, picked up a three-year-old boy who had fallen into the primate exhibit, "cradled" him, and turned him over to paramedics, experts reasoned that she must have imitated the nurturing acts of the zookeepers who raised her. Twenty years later, a similar accident happened at the Cincinnati Zoo. This time, Harambe, the gorilla who found himself faced with a human boy in his enclosure, was shot dead. If other animals are not unambiguously helping humans, they must be treated as direct threats.

Ultimately, what appears to be a selfless act must have hidden selfish benefits. What seemed like ravens sharing a feast by making a call that attracted more ravens to the scene—an incident extensively studied by Bernd Heinrich and which became the classic example of animal altruism—turned out to be merely juvenile ravens' strategy to protect themselves against a stronger, territory-holding rival.[6]

⌀

On a recent road trip, I began to reflect on the many "Deer [*sic*] in X miles" signs scattered across the United States. Besides depicting deers as potential hazards to humans simply by virtue of their existence, these warnings perpetuate a common view: that other-than-human beings amount to little more than fixtures in "nature," constituting an immovable part of their "habitat" and its "flora and fauna." How little physical mobility other animals have in the space that humans have claimed and come to dominate speaks to how little agency, individual and political, they are granted.

Indeed, as there is now no corner of "nature" that is untouched by humans, free-living animals who find themselves straddling the divide between *nature* and *civilization* are increasingly assimilated into our world, having to adapt to new food sources and ways of life. These include unwelcome visitors labeled as "pests," as well as free-living animals whom we have decided must live among us (against their will) if we are to give them special accommodations and institutionalized protection.

Such free-living animal species are increasingly confined within enclosures and reserves framed as conservation efforts. A supposedly nurturing "Mother Nature" (nature personified and feminized) now becomes an aggregate of impersonal forces and principles that prioritize the control and balancing of different populations and species without regard for individual welfare. This flipped narrative puts us in a position to decide what's best for other animals and their preservation. Boasting our ability to control and manipulate natural forces so we can artificially aid in the population increase of an endangered other-than-human species, we humans have decided that hunting, or the "sport" of killing for pleasure, falls under "conservation" and "population control." One must question the logic of breeding other-than-human animals in captivity specifically to be shot by an unnatural "predator," which in many cases is what happens. To caution against only "overhunting" and "overfishing" is to imply that we need only address the scale and methods of killing, not question the morality of killing in itself—a recurring theme in today's animal ethics.

Even the human practice of "hunting" and "shooting" other animals with cameras is, in practice, not innocuous. We seek out and corner other animals with the same arrogance and entitlement in order to capture them on film and extract knowledge about their ways of life that serves to reinforce our preconceived beliefs. Footage seen in nature documentaries, which often feed into our fascination with "exotic" beings who seem to live apart from our world, is not obtained without intrusion or great disturbance to the animals' homes. Production crews have been known to destroy nests and dens in trying to place their cameras, and staged killings are commonplace.

Not just deers or free-living animals but all other-than-human animals are relegated to neatly compartmentalized corners of our world—quarantined for our convenience or exploitation. Rats, mice, and rabbits are hidden in secluded laboratories, some even built underground. A plethora of laws and regulations determines where nonhuman companions or "service" animals can and can't go. The majority of other-than-human animals who exist on this planet—billions of fishes, cows, pigs, chickens, and turkeys—are shut away inside gargantuan "Concentrated Animal Farming Operations" (CAFOs).

There they are imprisoned. When Hurricane Florence was headed for the state of North Carolina in late 2018, Reuters ran an article with the headline AS HURRICANE NEARS, U.S. FARMERS RUSH TO CLEAR CROPS BUT ANIMALS *STAY* IN STORM'S PATH (emphasis added),[7] a conclusion the news agency reached when many farmers didn't even open up the gates to give the enslaved animals a fighting chance at survival. The thousands of pigs and millions of chickens who perished in the disaster simply became footnotes to the $1.1 billion in total "agricultural loss." You'll note that the Reuters headline suggests that the animals *chose* not to escape to safety as opposed to being unable to flee and that the farmers bore no responsibility for them, even though legally they were considered the farmers' "property." Interestingly, the language of agency shifted once the storm passed. Of those pigs and chickens who didn't die, many were "reclaimed" and "returned" to the facilities by farmers.

Our interactions with domesticated animals constitute an inherently unequal exercise of free will. Domestication is in itself an exchange of freedoms; while such an exchange could be voluntary and equitable (the Latin *domesticare*, from which "domestication" is derived, literally means "to dwell in a house," simply implying cohabitation), domestication of other animals has been disproportionately for the benefit of humans. We may have come to cohabit with some other-than-human animal species because both our and their ancestors ceded some agency long ago in order to gain from the mutual benefits. This origination story is still hotly debated, but it seems likely that that interdependence would have been lost soon after the first encounters.[8]

Indeed, when humans started breeding the friendliest members of certain species to be our companions, we might have been capitalizing on a grave genetic disadvantage: a new hypothesis posits that the impaired development of a group of cells called the neural crest cells, which underlies deficient adrenaline production, made the first domesticated animals less fearful of both the human strangers who approached them and potential sources of danger.[9]

It also seems to me bizarre the way we often infantilize domesticated nonhuman companions, even when they are fully grown adults or we don't know them personally. In addition to our tendency to value neotenic behaviors and physiognomies in other-than-human companions, we switch to a form of "baby talk" when addressing them (I'm certainly guilty of this from time to time, against my better judgment). Our infantilization extends to giving them less-than-dignifying, albeit cute, names like Fluffy or Fuzzy, which maintain the artificial distance between them and fully recognizable personhood. To complete the comparison of (adult) nonhuman companions to human children, human guardians often call their canine or feline companions their "babies," proclaiming themselves "parents." A number of recent articles report that millennials are increasingly choosing "fur kids" over human ones, implying that these two groups require interchangeable ethics of care. Other-than-human companions' status as permanent babies, compounded by our selective breeding for prized puppy-like characteristics and made all the more salient with casual phrases such as "good girl/

boy," "cute little thing," or "poor baby," prevent us from seeing them at eye level.

Even before they are born, today's domesticated animals have no choice but to forfeit their most basic claim to self-sufficiency and bodily and reproductive autonomy, as important decisions are constantly made for them. The mother cows who are forcibly impregnated, the male pigs who have their genitals mutilated to get rid of the "boar taint" (meaning to modify and purify the taste of their flesh), and the dogs and cats who have to be "fixed" (despite not being "broken") because of our long-running failure to curb the overpopulation of nonhuman companions—these are but a few of the species that suffer the consequences of the human gaze that reduces them to literal "pieces of meat" or "property." Unsurprisingly, denial of agency and self-autonomy, including reproductive freedom, figures into the narrative of oppression of not only other-than-human animals, but also many marginalized groups of humans.

It would serve us well to remember that many women of color have been forcibly experimented upon and sterilized in the past, that women's bodies continue to be policed in our healthcare system—that the "husband" or "daddy" stitch, for example, is an ongoing practice whereby doctors add a stitch in vaginal repair after childbirth, *without the woman's knowledge*, which supposedly increases her male partner's sexual pleasure.[10]

Let us not forget that state-sanctioned experimentation on unwilling humans, though no longer a reality, was a mainstay of dictatorial regimes: the Khmer Rouge operated on live humans—captured spies and enemies of the state—for "medical" purposes. Often, the same infrastructure that was used to confine and "manage" other-than-human animals conveniently doubled as an instrument to oppress vulnerable human beings. When the United States arrested and confined more than 100,000 Japanese Americans in internment camps during World War II, internees were kept in stables and stalls used for "livestock." Under the Third Reich, Jewish prisoners were packed tightly into cattle cars to be taken to concentration camps. When the Dachau gas chamber was built, SS doctor Sigmund Rascher proposed to try out a new war poison gas that had until then "been tested only on animals."

History tells us time and again that there is an extremely fine line between other-than-human and human oppression. In both cases, the same principle applies: individuals whose agency isn't fully recognized by the powers-that-be, who are said to not be able to think for themselves, also can't and don't need to give consent.

✪

Discursive violence against other-than-human animals goes further: not only are their very bodies mutated and cultivated as raw material and their bodily autonomy routinely violated, but the language used by industries and echoed by ordinary people positions other animals as passive beings who have things done to them rather than acting freely out of their own interests. In addition, when we use passive language, even to bring to light the suffering of individuals who were "raised in" certain abhorrent conditions or "subjected to" certain means of torture, the human perpetrators of that violence are absolved of all culpability.

A commonly held attitude is that other animals would be helpless and purposeless without humans. An industry manual on the "management of newborn calves" details the many weaknesses of the infant—breathing problems, insufficient nursing, and so on—which require the farmer to step in and provide assistance against their mother's judgment. An agronomy student once tried adamantly to convince me that he had witnessed mother cows on dairy farms stomping on their newborns. Again, I do not doubt that not all of those forced into motherhood can make for attentive mothers. But it's because of us that cows have been selectively bred for their milk-making and not parenting capacity (even their milk is fortified with minerals to suit adult humans' nutritional needs instead of the children of the cows); that they are imprisoned in environments that do not allow for healthy socialization and exchange of knowledge with their peers; and that they carry the trauma caused by multiple consecutive forced pregnancies. We are largely to blame.

In the same industry, "milking" becomes a form of human labor performed upon mother cows, a bodily function over which they can no longer assert autonomy; the various "products" that come from the white liquid are grouped under "dairy," a word originally used to refer to the building for making such "products." In the twenty-first century, this alienated labor has been further outsourced to mechanical vacuums attached to the cows' udders. The knowledge that cows don't produce milk year-round without being pregnant or nursing, or that sheeps, if left in their natural homes and not subjected to meddling by us, would all shed their wool themselves at the end of each winter, is suppressed in order to uphold the belief that human interference necessarily improves the lives of domesticated other-than-human animals.

In an article defending pig farmers' use of gestation crates that restrict individual movement and social interaction between sows, a farmer claims that these contraptions "keep the pigs safe from one another . . . [preventing] sows from . . . fights, which often cause injuries and sometimes even death [in nature]." The claim is that "trials have shown that given the choice, sows choose to be in those individual crates. . . . They prefer the comfort and security of not having to fight with other sows to get feed." One would almost believe that it's an accommodation for the pigs not to be able to move!

That we even have a debate over whether mother pigs would like to turn around at all shows how disconnected we are from what common sense tells us about the lives of those with whom we share analogous skins, flesh, and bones, as well as central nervous systems. Not coincidentally, other animals' preferences and needs invariably seem to align with what is most profitable for the industries that exploit them. The profit motive dictates that we deny other animals ownership of their suffering. We get to decide for them how much they suffer and what level of suffering is acceptable.

Humans exercise complete monopoly over the question of what needs other-than-human animals under our control have. Often, exploitative industries take steps to meet only the barest basic physical requirements for a living being to stay alive: minimum space, food, water, and medical care to hold them over until the day of slaughter or until their productivity expires, which is promptly followed by slaughter because there is no boundary between their life and use-value. Individualized mental enrichment or socialization needs are not considered. For the purposes of production, other-than-human animals are uncomplicated organic machines, operating on little more than a desire for pleasure or, as is more often the case in animal agribusiness, the avoidance of pain.

The myriad ways in which other-than-human animals are exploited constantly reproduce their dependency on humans. Many of them are bred and fed hormones specifically to be disabled. Chickens raised for meat ("broilers") become obese at six weeks of age; "layer" hens lay such an unnaturally large quantity of eggs that they end up with various reproductive cancers; and sheeps never stop growing wool and run the risk of suffocating in high temperatures. These disabilities are not merely tolerated but rather are intrinsic to higher productivity.[11]

As beings who, in their totality and at their fullest development, are compared by some, including activists, to incapacitated or incomplete humans, other-than-human animals can always stand to be "enhanced," either physically or cognitively, through genetic and surgical manipulation.[12]Against our own self-proclaimed core beliefs in bodily integrity and liberty, we have created Frankenstein-like creatures: from RoboRoaches (cockroaches with a device attached that interferes with their antenna nerves in order for "users" to remote-control their movement) to "double-muscled" pig mutants whose composition is made up of unusually large amounts of lean flesh.

☙

Not only is our tyranny framed as being in other-than-human animals' interest or "for their benefit," but we also lay claim to giving purpose to nonhuman lives, for without their usefulness to humans, a majority of them would not have been born. In our arrogance, we believe that other animals owe us their very existence: that they were destined to satisfy our fleeting desires for "steak," a fur coat, or an elephant ride. The cruelest irony of all is that many of us will then, either in earnest or for humorous effect, "thank the animal" for the life they didn't willingly give. Or, in praise of an exceptionally good meal, we might exclaim: "Those pigs did not die in vain!"

In 2017, in a controversial story, a farm in Wiltshire, United Kingdom, served up as a "token gesture" the flesh of a litter of eighteen piglets to the very firefighters who "rescued" them from a barn fire six months prior. Although news of the feast made more than a few readers uncomfortable, it merely made public what was implicitly understood, that the piglets, "whose bacon was saved" from the fire, were merely "given a six-month stay of execution when they were rescued," and it was "inevitable" that one day they would "go into the food chain." The farm's manager was quoted as saying: "You do feel sad at the end of it . . . but to bring them down for [the firefighters] was a good way of saying 'thank you.'"[13]

It's unfortunate that other-than-human animals are exploited for whatever humans can rob from their bodies, but for a few months leading up to the day of slaughter, at least they get to enjoy "the best quality of life"—so rationalizations such as the one above go. That is, if they're lucky: the fact remains that the majority of farms do not even claim to honor that promise of a good life. For those that do, whether reality lives up to their claim is another story.

To take the argument one step further, some claim that "at least the animals get to live at all." In *Man and the Natural World*, Keith Thomas traces this sentiment back to the eighteenth century, when "it was widely urged that domestication was good for animals; it civilized them and increased their numbers: 'we multiply life, sensation and enjoyment'" (quoting Benjamin Rush).[14] In a way, we fancy ourselves creators of other animals, which is not altogether different from men's long-running bid to claim for themselves all procreative power and, along with the exalted status of "authors of life," authority over women's bodies.

Obviously, this line of reasoning, like all other speciesist ones, stops short of being applied to humans. For us, bestowing life on someone doesn't justify any amount of abuse; our revulsion at such a stance either in theory or in practice and our condemnation of the abuse of children by their own parents reveal how thoroughly nonhuman lives have been cheapened by a speciesist double standard. Consumers who make this argument in a bid to take credit for helping to bring domesticated other-than-human animals into existence gloss over the fact that they simultaneously pay for the same individuals' immense suffering.

Paradoxically, whereas the overwhelming majority of other-than-human animals are socially and politically excluded from human society, they don't exist outside of the realm of our exploitation of them. Indeed, technological advancement is bringing us ever closer to the possibility of "phasing out" the use of other-than-human animals in vivisection or as "food." Our generation is one that has to seriously contemplate the possibility that the practice of breeding and exploiting other animals will become obsolete within our lifetime. We spend inordinate amounts of time simultaneously debating the questions "Will animals face extinction?" and "Will animals overrun the Earth?" Underlying these scenarios and inquiries, whether they are meant to be serious or jocular, is the sobering realization that there are entire species of beings to whom an existence free from enslavement is incomprehensible, and that we are so accustomed to exploiting them that their freedom is just as incomprehensible to us.

As such, we often represent other-than-human animals as willfully subservient to humans. Many advertisements on billboards, signs, or elsewhere feature self-cannibalizing or cannibalistic animals—individual animals in bibs, knives and forks in hand, who serve up their own flesh or the flesh of their own kind, who are complicit in their own exploitation or else are voluntarily participating in what seems like a mutually beneficial relationship. Many are even shown to be delighted by their usefulness to humans: the jubilant cartoon of the titular Laughing Cow on packages of cheese wedges was a mainstay of my childhood. The illusion of agency is extended to mice used in experiments who may be euphemistically called "research associates." Such perverse and misleading language may lead one to wonder if they should be entitled to workers' rights in the same way that dogs forced to run for "sport" might be considered eligible to receive compensation as "athletes."

This discursive subjugation is only a little too familiar: women, for example, know all too well what it's like to be portrayed in mainstream culture as tacitly asking to be overpowered—to subsequently take the blame when accounts of sexual harassment and sexual assault are rewritten in favor of their aggressors. In many of these depictions of other-than-human animals, they are replaced by cartoon versions of themselves or else are dead (I'm reminded of an advertisement that shows a dead chicken's body posed on all fours in a suggestive manner), because only then can they don human clothing or assume the often sexualized poses we want them to.

The infamous Chick-fil-A cows represent an interesting exception. The stars of the chain's wildly successful campaign, the cows, who carry signs bidding consumers to "Eat Mor Chikin," are obviously aware of their exploitation and have organized and taken action in protest—even if they are once more infantilized as poor spellers. Their agency is limited to silent protest in an attempt to shift the role of the target of exploitation from their own kind to another abused species. Ultimately, the consumer wields the power to decide their fate. The unusualness and intended hilarity, and by extension the success, of the campaign, lie in this false sense of agency displayed by the sign-wielding cows; Chick-fil-A has even created an annual Cow Appreciation Day and continues to take advantage of the occasion to sell more chickens' flesh.

Because the majority of other-than-human animals on Earth are trapped in systems that completely strip them of their agency, and thus the work of those who advocate for their rights involves physically liberating many of them from their current prisons, it is often easy even for these human allies to overlook other animals' agency. This is all the truer precisely because contrary to what we want to believe, our meddling in other animals' lives not only isn't by default positive but can in fact be extremely destructive in spite of our best intentions. The assumption of absolute human authority over other animals is one that needs examining even with respect to those who have come to depend on us, wholly or partially.

Once, on a road trip, I myself was forced to confront this dilemma when my travel partner and I came across a pit bull on the side of a highway eating "roadkill" and decided to take her to the local shelter. We later found out she was adopted within one day of being up for adoption following her holding period.

We could find out nothing about the family that took Honey, our name for her, but given the area we were traveling through and that she was a presumably abandoned pit bull with poorly cropped ears—all signs pointing to her past abuse—it was a very real possibility that she didn't go to the loving home we had hoped would be able to meet her needs.

For days afterward, I could not help but replay in my head the events of that day and the decisions we made on the spot that were fateful for Honey but that for us would eventually become a blur. I wondered whether her life might have been made worse by our taking it upon ourselves to "rescue" her from the streets under the simplistic assumption that she would be safer in the care of humans.

In sharing this anecdote, I don't mean to discourage anyone from taking action when they see an other-than-human individual in need. However, we should embrace the humility in recognizing that many circumstantial factors, in addition to human shortsightedness, complicate our definition of "rescue."

The rhetoric of "animal instinct," which paints "the animal" as a product of a blind, unconscious natural process distinct from human culture, both devalues and demonizes nonhuman agency, making our restraint and coercion of other animals justified. How to best help other animals regain agency in a world irreparably altered by humans and unrecognizable to them is not always obvious and a question that we should all take seriously, acting as their allies and not their saviors. This humility will only propel the movement for animal equity forward.

4

"Like an Animal"

How Language Takes Away Power

ACCORDING TO A 2011 HARRIS POLL, 90 PERCENT OF AMERICANS who live with other-than-human companions think of their dogs and cats as members of the family. Yet, as far as business owners, the government, the law, and pretty much the rest of human society are concerned, their beloved family members are classified as property, many subject to "obedience training." The myriad signs in public spaces and in front of businesses addressed to "dog owners" tell them to "clean up after their dogs," "keep their dogs on a leash at all times," or that their canine companions can't be in that space at all. These individuals' fundamental status as property means that, although they are among the lucky few who may be kept in our homes, protected and even pampered, they remain in the same precarious position in human society as all other-than-human animals.

Human bias against other animals creates fundamentally unequal power relations, the most obvious manifestation of which is that almost all relationships between humans and domesticated animals are framed as ones of ownership. We readily recognize some other-than-human animals as our companions, family members even—people who listen to our troubles and share our joys—but the particularities of these relationships aren't usually of much interest to people beyond who the human responsible for an other-than-human person is. We subject those individuals to a softer exercise of control, but an exercise of control nonetheless.

In many jurisdictions, mistreatment of other-than-human animals, even companions, may be prosecuted as "property damage," the plaintiffs here being the human "owners." Even when the "owners" themselves are abusive, law enforcement may fail to seize the abused other-than-human persons precisely because a human's right to property trumps an other-than-human animal's right to freedom from harm. And the convention of eschewing relational nouns when referring to an other-than-human animal companion in favor of simply "my dog" or "her cat" highlights how we have normalized the idea that someone's very being can be made into a possession.

Furthermore, forcible ownership of other animals is so deeply rooted in human history that the concept is built into many common terms today. "Stock," as in "livestock," had since the early fifteenth century been used to mean "sum of money" or "supply for future use"; the more precise meaning of "movable property of a farm" emerged in the early sixteenth century. "Cattle," which shares an etymological development with "chattel," derives from the Latin *capitale* meaning "property" or "stock," itself a derivation of *capitalis*, literally "of the head," as in "head of cattle." For millennia, animals labeled as "cattle" have been made synonymous with wealth, with devastating consequences. Yet the gravity of calling an entire section of other-than-human animals a term that signifies "living inventory" still evades many advocates. Even social media star Esther the Wonder Pig, arguably the most well-known pig on the Internet, one who has helped so many humans see the complexity and diversity of a species so often dismissed, was initially refused cancer treatment because she was considered "food."[1] Not only that, but articles covering her story consistently referred to her two human fathers as her "owners."

Discourse based on ownership reinforces in symbolic terms humans' actual dominance over other animals, as well as the sense of entitlement with which we regard their bodies as a source of consumption. According to Arran Stibbe, the power exerted over other animals is completely coercive: they do not consent to their treatment, and they are neither aware of the ideological violence against them reenacted in discourse, nor able to counter it.[2]

Not only are other-than-human animals not allowed to protest their treatment, but the assumption has indeed always been that they can't. We have successfully silenced other animals' voices so that we get to write and rewrite not only their individual stories but also entire narratives of human–other animal relationships. In doing so, we further keep them trapped at the bottom of the power hierarchy, the power we assert over other animals being both interpersonal and institutional.

The "humane meat" movement has, with great success, taken advantage of discourse and images of "happy" other-than-human animals to shift the blame and focus completely away from the problems that persist even on so-called humane farms and onto CAFOs or "factory farms." CAFOs have now been largely stigmatized in the public imagination, so much so that even if one isn't overtly opposed to them—the worst of the worst inventions in animal agribusiness—one at least cannot publicly proclaim one's support.

Although "humane meat" advocates and the corporations that capitalize on this marketing scheme claim to be dedicated to protecting farmed animals and improving their lives, they neglect to mention that the supposed differences between their advertised improvements and "standard industry practices," which no matter how gruesome are rarely questioned, carry little meaning. The only consistent result of a push to more "humane" standards is that consumers can now continue buying products derived from the bodies of other-than-human animals without as much guilt, or even feel virtuous or pleased about paying for labels such as FREE-RANGE, CAGE-FREE, GRASS-FED, VEGETARIAN-FED, and so on.

As more documentation of the gross mistreatment of other-than-human animals inside remote and windowless facilities surfaces and becomes widely accessible, and as we come to find out more about the inner lives of other animals, various companies are changing their strategies to appeal to consumers who want to make ethical choices. The promises they make based on ethical principles, however, prove largely superficial. Many of the same companies that take the lives of thousands of other-than-human individuals each day now claim to champion the obligation to ensure the "health and well-being of the animals" under their control.[3]

Without fail, these companies all insist that they partner with only "small family farms" and that they care about "their animals." They may even produce commercials or offer virtual farm tours that take the viewer directly onto one of these farms, where the animals are all said to have individual names. Equally ironic is the industry's harnessing of facial recognition technology, a technology that forces one to recognize other-than-human animals' unique features and needs, ultimately to "systematize the cost of feed" for each individual and determine "when it's the right time to sell," or to minimize loss by identifying disease before it spreads among closely confined individuals—in other words, to optimize production.[4]

Petco, which has been exposed for sourcing the "pets" it sells from a horribly abusive supplier that is likely only one of many, advertises fishes on its website by noting "natural variations in each species" and that "[e]ach companion animal is different in shape, color, and personality." That Petco apparently recognizes the intra-species diversity of the fishes it puts up for sale is not enough to stop the company from applying the same price tag to all guppies, betta fishes, or goldfishes.

Even animal advocates, for all their commitment to justice and equity for all beings, fall into the trap of always speaking *for* other-than-human animals and treating them as a powerless group. Many of them appeal to the public by imploring it to act as a "voice for the voiceless." Whereas industries and individuals who seek to exploit other-than-human animals capitalize on a narrative of stewardship and benevolent control, organizations and activists fighting *for* animal equity employ one of abuse and victimization. Although the goals of the two groups could not be more different, both exercise the human privilege of imposing their desired narratives onto other animals. Further, much of today's advocacy discourse presents a somewhat dramatized view of other animals, especially domesticated animals, as innocent and trusting—gentle beings who would not do to us what we do to them even if given the chance. I understand the goal is to tap into suppressed empathy for animal species other than our own, but perhaps this rhetoric also serves to reiterate our belief that other animals have internalized helplessness— to assuage our fear of the ruthless "animalistic" force that, like the saying "eat or be eaten," threatens to usurp our power. This thinking remains squarely embedded in human supremacy.

❧

When other animals are featured in our cultural narratives, they more often than not take the forms of caricatured or stylized representations based on stereotypes. Some are exaggerations of actual aspects or behaviors of other animals that we've observed; many stereotypes, however, are beliefs not based in observation. Other-than-human animals frequently make an appearance in allegories, fables, fairytales, idioms, expressions, and even insults (the ultimate manifestation of our tendency to project the most undesirable human qualities onto those other beings from whom we can maintain a safe distance). Human speech and writing always make liberal use of other animals as metaphors, to condemn and deride as well as to admire and praise. Whether a species' portrayal is predominantly negative or positive is often indicative of its status in the human-imposed order of the natural world.

Portrayals of other-than-human animals in the media sometimes go a long way toward popularizing or solidifying stereotypes with which they are associated: for example, Disney's 1942 film *Bambi* characterizes deers as naïve, fragile animals. The same is true of culturally influential texts. The Bible warns: "Beware of false prophets, who come to you in sheep's [*sic*] clothing but inwardly are ravenous wolves (Matthew 7:15 NRSV)." Similarly, in one of the fables credited to Ancient Greek storyteller Aesop, the foolish sheeps, being too trusting of the wolves, dismissed the guard dogs who protected them, only to be subsequently made supper of. Today, Americans tend to think of sheeps as gullible, snakes as untrustworthy, cows as unintelligent (though these species may represent completely different character traits in other cultures), and so on.

On the other hand, specific positive qualities, such as physical dexterity and prowess, of (often carnivorous) totemic species such as tigers and eagles are highlighted in their representations as sports team mascots, as the sidekicks of fictional human superheroes, or as the models for their superhuman powers. Regardless of their origins, once these tropes have entered mainstream culture as widely recognized stereotypes of other-than-human animals, they tend to be evoked in everyday discourse and media as a kind of shorthand for expressing particular qualities, and are frequently accepted without question.

Oftentimes, stories with other-than-human animal characters serve to highlight various aspects of the human experience or to extol what we believe to be exclusively human virtues. Movies such as *Okja* or *Free Willy* celebrate the courage of human protagonists willing to take risks to ensure an other-than-human animal's freedom. Ironically, the whale who "starred" in the latter film died only a year and a half after being returned to his true home, where he remained dependent on humans until his passing. His tragic story points to the shared fate of many an other-than-human "actor" when the cameras stop rolling.

Even when they play the role of protagonists, however, other-than-human animals are still romanticized or "cutefied" so as to make them fit for human consumption, both figuratively and literally. They become the animated characters we see in children's movies or are featured in Internet memes and funny clips meant to be daily pick-me-ups. They are rendered into trivial entertainment. This abstraction explains why we can root for, say, the main characters in the 2000 animated movie *Chicken Run*—a group of chickens living on a "meat" farm who plan and successfully execute a plan to escape slaughter—while at the same time, Burger King can advertise its kids' meals with toy characters from the same movie franchise. Unsuspecting youngsters were happily gobbling up "nuggets" of the flesh of their favorite characters.

The fluidity with which other-than-human animals pass from beloved fictional characters (metaphorical source of consumption) to "food" (literal source of consumption) was further made clear to me in a Facebook post I recently came across—a picture of minced "ham" jokingly captioned "Peppa Pig jigsaw puzzle." (Peppa Pig is a well-known British kids' show animated character.) It is a chillingly apt caption that speaks to the fragmentation of other-than-human bodies as both real and hypothetical beings.

Clearly, the ability of cinema and narrative as a medium to elicit sympathy for other-than-human animal characters does not necessarily constitute an education in cross-species understanding; movies can star inanimate objects as protagonists with equal success. Notably, the 2016 animated dark comedy *Sausage Party* revolves around an anthropomorphized sausage trying to escape being eaten by humans. The logic of animating someone's flesh that is already dead and processed beyond recognition rather than the live individual is absurd, but *Sausage Party* is no more absurd than advertising images of anthropomorphized and sexualized burgers and nuggets showing off their cleavage and behinds.

Other-than-human animals are thus not treated as inherently meaningful but become vehicles of human stories and human-assigned meaning; this is called metaphorical borrowing in Carol J. Adams's *The Sexual Politics of Meat*. So despite the high visibility of representations of other animals as TV and movie characters, the fickle empathy that we readily profess toward these other-than-human animals who have been repackaged into metaphorical beings does not translate easily to their real-life counterparts. We may enjoy the occasional headline about a bull who managed to escape from a transport truck on the way to his death, and may even admire and applaud the audacious resister. However, we are generally unwilling to challenge the violent institutions that drove the individual to such desperation in the first place.

The idea that other animals may have the capacity to meaningfully self-organize and resist human oppression is to us at once absurd and terrifying, because we would then be forced to acknowledge our own tyranny. Fred, a goat "fugitive" who escaped from auction in New Jersey and reportedly "[roamed] the town at night with deer [*sic*]" for more than a year, made headlines when rumors surfaced that he played a role in helping seventy-five other animals escape from the same auction house. Even as his story of resistance and heroism gained the support of many, Fred was eventually captured and returned to his "owner."[5]

❂

In a valuation system devised and controlled by humans, other animals' lives only hold as much value as their usefulness to humans. We devise a different use and price tag for all the beings with whom we cross paths, branding entire groups of individuals as "broiler" or "layer chickens," "veal calves," "fur seals," and "emotional support" or "food" animals. The way in which we treat even members of the same species depends greatly on whether they are considered "food," "pets," or "research subjects."

In many ways, far and long removed from the actual existence of other-than-human animals, the otherness associated with *animality*—fully expressed in other animals and repressed in ourselves—remains a product of human imagination. This otherness is a sociocultural construction in which other animals, in their othered position, have no say.[6]

As much as they are already devalued in life, in death other-than-human animals are subjected to even more violence. Their bodies are skinned, defeathered, cut up, and neatly packaged until they are no longer recognizable as having body parts. Upon death, other animals' bodies undergo a transformation that ours do not. Each individual's bodily integrity disintegrates. The flesh of multiple chickens is ground up together as "nuggets"; "sausages" cannot be traced back to individual pigs, nor "patties" to individual cows, whence originated the infamous phrase "mystery meat."

In fact, given how companies often go the extra mile to reassure consumers of the conditions in which "their [referring to the consumers] meat was raised," not only is the live, intact, other-than-human victim completely absent in this rhetoric, but the possession of their "processed" body parts has been transferred to potential buyers even before the transaction of the "product" necessarily takes place.

This is in stark contrast to humans, who have the choice to become organ donors and can dictate in their wills what they want done with their bodies after death. In other words, we retain bodily autonomy even when we no longer have any use for our bodies. I am reminded of the moving story of a father who traveled thousands of miles to meet the recipient of his deceased daughter's heart and listen to the heartbeat for the last time through a stethoscope. Even post-transplant, we collectively continue to remember and treasure donated organs as once belonging to selfless donors, even as they now function in different bodies.

Even when other social taboos (such as cannibalism, for instance) are broken, the belief that a human corpse never truly loses its identity endures. When the Evil Queen devours what she believes to be Snow White's vital organs, it is in order to absorb the latter's youth and beauty. When Europeans, who by the sixteenth century were consuming ground-up human corpses as medicine (all the while calling their cultural enemies "cannibals" and "giants," deeming them uncivilized for not being able to distinguish between humans and the animals fit to become food), it was not so much their nutrient composition but the "vitality of life" or the spirit of the dead that constituted the healing properties of these remedies.[7]

Most other animals, with the exception of select companions to humans, aren't afforded the same euphemisms for death as we are. Instead of simply dying, we "pass away," and our deaths are always characterized as losses. On the other hand, to say that a group of humans has been "slaughtered like animals" is to describe one of the greatest crimes against humanity—the devaluation of humanity itself. The loss of nonhuman lives, even as collateral damage, is reduced to "bycatch," "roadkill," "trash animals" (non-target animals caught in fur traps), and so on. From these emotionless, unflowery terms, one can glean only the basic pieces of information—the place or cause of their deaths.

❦

We force ourselves upon other animals figuratively and literally, granting ourselves ready access to their bodies. The consequences of this entitlement range from mild annoyance on the part of the other-than-human subjects of our attention (who are petted or approached without having indicated to us their expressed desire or consent) to outright physical harm. Those who physically resist our intrusion on their personal spaces are deemed "aggressive," and if by chance a human fails to heed their message and gets hurt, they run the risk of being punished or even killed. There is no dearth of stories of humans who take their entitlement to the bodies of nonhuman others to the extreme, who place lit fireworks in dogs' mouths, burn chickens to death, or torture insects for their own amusement.

We are oblivious to the sheer burden caused by our unsolicited attention and expectation of accessibility, however well-meaning our intentions. Even in the realm of advocacy, each other-than-human animal is expected to act as a friendly ambassador who can represent their group and articulate its plight. These emissaries are obligated to embody a story that is easily digestible for outsiders, such that activists sometimes feel the need to oversimplify their experiences. Each anonymous face on a flyer or billboard has to be "cute" or palatable enough to elicit our sympathy. For many other-than-human animals, from the rare white tiger to the "common" pug—both of whom are victims of inbreeding for certain physical characteristics, resulting in disabilities and lifelong health complications—aesthetic value at the expense of quality of life is what is exchanged for what we deem acceptable care and protection of them.

In truth, many other-than-human animals, even those who are domesticated, have no desire to interact with humans, let alone to be totally dependent on us—a realization I arrived at as I watched a group of chickens go about their business, completely ignoring my existence. In my mind, such experiences more than cast doubt on the oft-told narrative that frames all instances of domestication as symbiotic exchanges.

Unsatisfied with admiring the beauty of "exotic" other-than-human species from afar, we rip them from their homes, strip them of their freedom, and deprive them of contact with their species kin. The "admiration" that drives our desire to possess them makes them go mad—pacing the length of their jail cells, gnawing at the metal bars—just so we can enjoy a trip to the zoo or SeaWorld, or watch elephants perform when the circus comes to town. These industries try to tell us that the experience can only be "educational," inspiring in wide-eyed children a love and respect for nature and other animals, even as they rob the same individuals of everything that is natural and important to them.

We even have the presumption to declare that captivity keeps other-than-human animals from danger. Daring zoo breakouts are thus often framed as silly antics and fodder for, at best, amusing anecdotes. In 2016, Kali, a seven-year-old orangutan confined at Kansas City Zoo, "grabbed glass panes" that separated her from zoo visitors and "pulled herself 14 feet to the top [of the wall]." After she "got a brief taste of freedom" (note the irony of this word choice), however, Kali was said to "[climb] back down into the exhibit."[8] Even when escaped zoo inmates do not willingly return but are recaptured, they are often said to have been found "safe and well." The sad truth is that for many other-than-human animals, humans pose the greatest danger, be it directly or indirectly by means of environmental destruction.

No matter how gross our appropriation of other animals' bodies, the narrative that has survived to this day is that this violation is *normal, natural,* and *necessary.*

My childhood memories, for one, are colored with images of cartons of strawberry- and orange-flavored yogurt drinks, a wildly popular break-time or after-school snack for Vietnamese schoolchildren of my generation. Our naïve belief that dairy was the only or best source of calcium was reinforced from all directions, from concerned family members to the Vietnamese government, which in 2013 championed a failed initiative to increase the average height of the population by funding free milk in nurseries and primary schools. Many Vietnamese also still swear by imported infant formula, even though it's made from the lowest-quality whey—the leftover dried liquid from cheesemaking, originally a waste product of dairy industries in the West. And, in any case, more than 90 percent of East and Southeast Asians are thought to be lactose intolerant.

That eating other animals is a natural rather than cultural phenomenon in view of our evolutionary history is at the core of perhaps the most common defense of speciesism. Our attachment to this practice is in large part based on the belief that it was and is responsible for the development of our "advanced" intelligence. To call a human who consumes other animals an "omnivore" or even "carnivore" is greatly misleading, for these labels turn what is an ethical discussion into one about humans' natural diet based on our physiology. For animal advocates to, on the other hand, spend so much time arguing that eating other animals' flesh is unnatural or that we are the only species that drinks another's milk is to legitimize a largely moot debate that overshadows broader ethical questions about our relationships with the rest of animalkind. Although the term "carnism," coined by Dr. Melanie Joy in her book *Why We Love Dogs, Eat Pigs, and Wear Cows* to describe the "invisible belief system" in which "eating certain animals is considered ethical and appropriate,"[9] refocuses our attention onto an ideology, the very terminology remains tied to diet. I find the term still less comprehensive than "speciesism."

As many new vegans soon realize, they are "vegan in a non-vegan world," in which the exploitation of nonhuman persons for human benefit is very much the norm. It is simply something that has always been this way. Every leap of human history has been built on the literal backs of other animals— from ancient battles fought on horses' bodies to the emergence of the intensive "livestock production" that characterized the Industrial Revolution. The argument of necessity (whether economic, cultural, or scientific) for the continued "sourcing" and "harvesting" of other-than-human bodies as resources to fuel human civilization is legitimized by sterile industry jargon.

In "animal research" (as opposed to "vivisection"), other-than-human subjects are "administered" different substances or "exposed" to different "stimuli." In animal "agriculture," piglets who have their heads bashed open with a hammer are said to undergo "blunt force trauma," an acceptable and "humane" method of killing. Thus, challenges to these industries are often derisively dismissed as attacks against science, agriculture, and even the economy and human progress as a whole. In countering these accusations, activists may get sidetracked by the same industry-specific terminology and logic—arguing, for example, that high "feed conversion ratios" make animal "farming" "inefficient" and "unsustainable"—thus entertaining a speciesist narrative.

Perhaps most insidious of all is the cultural conditioning that inures us to the ubiquity and mundaneness of "animal products," including those of us who choose not to consume them. We don't think twice about words such as "meat" and "milk," which have come to be associated almost exclusively with the flesh and secretions of other-than-human animals, even though "meat" comes from an Old English root meaning simply "food" or "nourishment," and the use of "milk" to refer to plant juices and saps goes as far back as the 1200s. As a recent demonstration by People for the Ethical Treatment of Animals (PETA) Australia amply showed, the sight of a dog being cooked and eaten—even a synthetic one—can cause outrage among the general public and vegetarians and vegans alike,[10] but few of us even flinch when we walk past the "meat" counter at the grocery store. One is just a more socially acceptable form of the same act of killing.

☙

In Western society, "human" and "animal" are loaded political identities that have historically served as a gatekeeping tool, especially from the sixteenth and seventeenth centuries onward, to restrict institutional power to one particular group. To be fully human was (and in many ways still is) to be a cisgender, heterosexual male, neurotypical and able-bodied, wealthy, and white. Once again, this definition excludes from human society and the realm of human moral concern not only other-than-human animals but also entire sections of the human population. To victimize any group of humans and instill a sense of shame in their beings, it often suffices to push them toward the category of "animal."

When Donald Trump Jr. made the incendiary remark that evoked one's ability to "enjoy a day at the zoo" to defend the construction of a border wall to presumably protect Americans from "illegal immigrants,"[11] the eyebrow-raising analogy nevertheless made clear that in both instances, physical barriers serve to reinforce mental demarcations erected between ourselves and all the "others," to keep them at arm's length physically and metaphorically.

Those who are in positions of power often fancy themselves benevolent wielders of it. In his 1899 poem "The White Man's Burden," Rudyard Kipling elevated colonial conquests to a noble enterprise, a noxious notion that was an expression of and a spur to American imperialism. To Kipling, "uncivilized" peoples—the "barbarians" and "savages," "[y]our new-caught, sullen peoples, / Half-devil and half-child"—depended on the white imperialist to lead them to industrialization and cultural and religious enlightenment. Kipling exhorted his American readers to "[t]ake up the White Man's burden" in order "[t]o seek another's profit, / And work another's gain." The reverse was true: the imperialist had the most to gain from the enterprise of empire.

With the emergence of the "new science" of the seventeenth century, empirical backing for our self-proclaimed absolute authority over the natural world legitimized the biblical notion of "dominion" over other animals, even when in practice "dominion" was taken more and more to mean the right to exploit and despoil. Just as nineteenth-century Americans came to believe in a "Manifest Destiny" that justified white settlers' expansion across the continent, leaving a trail of theft and genocide in their wake, our relationship with other animals in the modern era was now elevated to a delusional mission to "redeem" and improve upon the animal kingdom "by high example."[12] Like "nature" itself, other-than-human beings remain neutral and useless until transformed through domestication by humans and through other anthropogenic alterations of their livelihoods. Farmers have protected sheeps from the Big Bad Wolf since the fairy tales of yore, so it was then, as now, "best for the beasts that they should be under man."[13] Today, captive breeding programs are saving or even bringing "endangered" species back from the brink of extinction. Perhaps the goal is well-intentioned and not purely aesthetic; it is possible that recovering a particular "endangered" species would bring broader benefits to other individuals in the same ecosystem. However, I think it's important to realize that it is supremely arrogant of us to decide whether it is justified to prioritize the longevity of an abstract collective entity (the "endangered" species) and the viability of its hypothetical future members over the well-being of existent members, who are being held captive.

In any given era, the dominant group has maintained its elevated position of power by claiming complete control of the social and moral hierarchy. Biological difference, real and imagined, is often used to cement this status ranking. The human penchant throughout history for naming, categorizing, and ranking everything and everyone in sight is not an uncomplicated and harmless eccentricity. Naming and classification are political acts; they symbolize a crucial manifestation of power—the ability to dictate how the world is represented and perceived by others.[14]

In the nineteenth century, physician and craniologist Samuel George Morton amassed the world's largest pre-Darwinian collection of human skulls from all races. Morton subsequently ranked these racial groups by cranial capacity, which he used as a rough index of overall intelligence. The results were as any of his contemporaries would anticipate—whites were superior to Native Americans, with blacks at the bottom—and were welcomed in an age when few people of European descent doubted their innate superiority; finally, here was hard fact to replace idle belief. Later reinterpretation of Morton's data, however, showed "apparently unconscious finagling" and that skulls of all races have approximately equal capacities.[15]

A ranked classification of the animal kingdom, which is still in use today, was undertaken in the eighteenth century by Carl

Linnaeus, a European biologist from a wealthy background (only the well-to-do had the time to study natural history and memorize thousands of Latin names for every known species). Although Linnaean taxonomy correctly places humans alongside other animals, *Homo sapiens* or "man of wisdom"—the nomenclature that Linnaeus gave to our species—is still at the very top of his classification and distinguishes humans from even the other members of the "highest" class of animals, *Mammalia*.

It's no coincidence that of all the unique characteristics of the class he designated mammals, Linnaeus chose the presence of milk-producing breasts (*mammae*) to be its defining feature. The implication is that this female characteristic is what "ties humans to brutes, while a traditionally male characteristic (reason) marks our separateness."[16] Linnaeus believed in a strict hierarchical order of all organisms; he also did not fail to separate the human species into four categories—*Europaeus*, *Americanus*, *Asiaticus*, and *Africanus*—"white Europeans" being the most civilized and most "human."

As Marjorie Spiegel writes in *The Dreaded Comparison*, "Let us remember that to the oppressors, there is often very little difference between one victim and the next."[17] Both disenfranchised humans and other-than-human animals have always served as pawns in humanity's game of power. That the boundaries between them are often treated as porous is once again confirmed through the language of slurs and insults. The use of "bitch," "sow," and "shrew," just to name a few, thinly veils the speaker's contempt for women; the term "chick," although not outright hostile, still infantilizes at the same time as it animalizes. Meanwhile, black people have historically been likened to "apes," "chimpanzees," and "monkeys."[18]

In the oppressors' eyes, marginalized humans and other-than-human animals are metaphorically interchangeable; aspects of human and other animal lives are cherry-picked and co-opted with equal frequency and aggressiveness. The Uncle Remus stories, vernacular trickster narratives largely derived from African folktales that were brought to the "New World" and retold by black slaves, chronicle the exploits of "Br'er Rabbit" and other "creeturs" who speak "de same ez folks." These characters inspired many a white children's author, including Beatrix Potter and A. A. Milne, to later build upon the tradition of turning American minstrelsy into animal fables.

P. L. Travers's first Mary Poppins novel, published in 1934, introduces readers to a scantily clad "negro lady" dandling "a tiny black pickaninny" (an offensive term for a black child) and addressing Mary Poppins in minstrel dialect. Travers was pressured to drop the racialized dialogue, and by the time of the 1981 revision, the "negro lady" had become a hyacinth macaw. According to Travers, black children loved reading the "pickaninny dialect" in her book; she made the changes only to appease meddlesome parents. Meanwhile, Disney's 1941 *Dumbo* features a crow literally named Jim Crow, voiced by a white actor "talkin' jive."[19]

Not only racist, sexist, and other discriminatory epithets but general insults also often rely on animal imagery: they casually and liberally reference pigs, cows, snakes, rats, sheeps, and donkeys, among others. The names of other-than-human animal species come to signify by themselves various negative traits: we have adjectives such as "cocky," "chicken," and "snaky" as well as verbs such as "ape" and "parrot." The word "ass" comes from the Latin *asinus* meaning both "donkey" and "idiot"; regardless of which sense preceded the other, the association persists because our view of neurologically deviant humans remains not separate from, but fundamentally bound up with, our view of nonhuman otherness.

I doubt many actually think snakes are inherently disloyal, or pigs are inherently chauvinist or uncultured. (In any case, the phrase "uncultured swine" privileges only an anthropocentric definition of "culture.") Even if in reality the other-than-human individuals whose names we've turned into gratuitous pejoratives don't embody the despised human traits that we project onto them, caricatures of the "deceitful" fox, the "dumb" mule, and the "filthy" pig endure in our collective imagination. Growing up, I used to be reprimanded for leaving my room "like a pigsty"; indeed, exact equivalents of many disparaging sayings in English about other animals exist in Vietnamese and probably many other languages. Just as manifestations of nonhuman exploitation in different cultures can converge, contempt for particular other-than-human animals can transcend cultural boundaries.

A dog-loving Western audience may be shocked to discover, however, that many Vietnamese insults evoke dogs. The species name itself is "credited with potency"—that is, it functions as a standalone insult—in the case of *thằng chó* ("you dog") or *đồ chó cái* ("bitch"). Unlike in English, there is rarely any ambiguity in the intended meaning when someone is called a "dog," female or not. Other usages such as *chó ghẻ* ("mange-afflicted dog"), *chó hoang* ("stray dog"), *chó vô chủ* ("ownerless dog"), or *chó chui gầm chạn* ("cowering dog") ironically point to conditions caused by neglect or mistreatment by humans. However, this cultural difference in language involving our canine friends is not an absolute rule: Donald Trump's long history of hurling unconventional canine-inspired insults at his adversaries ("choked like a dog," "sweat like a dog," "firing that dog") is proof that adoration for dogs does not extend everywhere, even within a culture that affords protection to many members of the species. Indeed, no species appears to be completely untouched by our colorful repertoire of invectives.

Violence against other-than-human animals is further normalized and trivialized through the use of everyday idiomatic expressions such as "more than one way to skin a cat," "beat a dead horse," or "kill two birds with one stone." English has an expansive repertoire of at least 25,000 idioms, which serve as windows into how humans of centuries past used to live even as they shape our present lives and the legacy we are leaving behind. Indeed, the activities described by some of the most common idioms may be outdated and even illegal today. They may no longer align with our ethics (a person saying "have a dog in the fight" may very well be vehemently against dogfighting in practice). We may not even understand the original references in many of these phrases. That we are willing to accept these pervasive linguistic artifacts and their content as collective memory and social scripts without any critical examination is alarming.

Due to their ubiquity and embeddedness in the English language, speciesist idioms are often mistaken for harmless, universally understood and accepted sayings. Not only that, those who propose animal-friendly alternatives are often promptly ridiculed and dismissed as "too sensitive." Mainstream culture's pathologizing of humans who care about other animals as being not only socially but also psychologically abnormal is nothing new; several late nineteenth-century physicians explained such bizarre behavior as "zoophilpsychosis" (an excessive concern for other-than-human animals). Women, who have been in the majority within the animal advocacy movements in the United Kingdom and the United States since the nineteenth century, were "particularly susceptible to the malady" and more likely to receive a diagnosis.[20] To this day, the movement for nonhuman liberation is caricatured as a phenomenon rooted in emotion. It's utterly ironic that a society that should be concerned by its shortage of empathy chooses instead to decry its excess.

❂

At the end of the day, we humans share a fundamental vulner-ability with other animals precisely by virtue of our animality. We have flesh and bones that are exposed to physical forces and neural structures that are alterable by psychological abuse. We are vulnerable to violence, both structural and interpersonal, and affronts to our personal identities. Oppressed bodies, regardless of species, may be manipulated, distorted, disfigured, or recon-figured to be at the service of the oppressors—to be literally and symbolically consumed. In the 2017 science fiction psychological horror *Get Out*, black bodies serve as literal empty vessels for white consciousness—the transplanted brains of white people. Tellingly, the recurring image of a buck's mounted head in the film acts as a symbol of white dominance over the black male ("buck" is a known post-Reconstruction racial slur for black men who refused to acquiesce to white authority figures), who like the other-than-human victim is reduced to a "trophy."[21]

It is this recognition of shared vulnerability that has compelled many activists from historically marginalized communities to bring each of their uniquely powerful retellings of personal and intergenerational trauma to bear on the experiences of the other-than-human animals whose bodies are "grown" and "harvested" for human use. At the same time, there is a considerable ambivalence and even an unwillingness to acknowledge this shared narrative of oppression at risk of perpetuating the animalization of folks who already struggle to be recognized as fully human.

To that end, the conversation about institutionalized violence against other-than-human animals still largely abstains from referring to them as "victims" and "survivors"; it omits terms with universally recognizable gravity such as "massacre," "sexual assault" or "rape," and "enslavement." In the 1970s, psychologist Harry Harlow, who was isolating rhesus macaque monkeys to induce in them clinical depression, devised what he himself called a "rape rack" to force female "isolates" to have children and to test their parenting skills. Despite being of a different species, I speak from my experience of femaleness when I say that I would struggle to find a way to adequately frame the trauma undergone by these monkeys without using the very terminology that seemed to be blatantly and thoroughly embraced by their human oppressor. Although experiential differences no doubt exist, the power dynamics that enable sexual violence against human and other animal victims are shared.

Whereas it's seen as taboo and "trivializing" to extend the language of human tragedies to other animals, damning descriptions of humans being "treated like animals" speak to the unimaginable level of contempt and violence displayed by a fellow human toward another. That the parallels between acts of violence against humans and those against other animals only work unidirectionally in popular discourse is again indicative of a fundamental power differential. As philosopher Paul Bloom suggests, the "sadism of treating human beings like [other animals] lies precisely in the recognition that they are not," that they would be ashamed to be thought of and treated this way.[22] Anthropocentric self-awareness is not easily extinguishable—indeed, it may be accentuated—by the cruelty of a fellow human being.

It is then all the more difficult to see, as I have in my own home country, that many of the practices we now consider normal—keeping "pets" (especially purebred ones) exclusively for companionship and spending disposable income on them, following a diet heavy in "meat" and "dairy," wearing fur, and so on—are "marks of new money." Or they are ways for communities and countries that are just now overcoming historical trauma and economic setback to reclaim comforts that were withheld from them by the rich, white slaveholders and imperialists of the past.

*

The prevalence of the "us versus them" mentality and the aggression born of this attitude are not in the least bit enigmatic. One might reason that an innate need to belong and to be able to navigate our social environment with ease comes with our socialness as a species. Thus, individual members pledge allegiance to a particular group in order to enhance their self-image and foster their sense of belonging. On the other hand, perhaps they find it most advantageous to align themselves with the group to bolster their competitiveness in the endless race to secure scarce resources. Either of these motives might indeed lead to an exaggerated perception of similarities within one's own group and differences between theirs and other groups, from which stereotyping of the "other" might arise.

Thus prejudice may start out benign enough—as the preferential treatment of one's own group rather than direct hostility toward other groups; one need not imply the other.[23] It is unevenly distributed personal and institutional power that generates perceived threats to the dominant group's privileged position and acts as the mechanism that translates prejudiced mental states into actual discrimination against human and other-than-human communities. Our eagerness to guard the boundaries of our own social group and reluctance to open the gates and admit another (or *an "other"*) as "one of us" are feelings of anxiety that, when empowered and acted upon, create social disparities. At best, they limit our ability to effectively expand our moral community in slower, incremental steps toward inclusion.

Through a monopoly on meaning and narrative, we are able to exercise power over other animals discursively as well as physically. In the interest of maintaining this power and the concomitant privileges, we continue to devalue other animals, deny them meaningful participation in their relationships with us, and disregard their ownership of their very bodies and capacity to determine their destinies.

The movement for nonhuman liberation is not only a call to recognize other-than-human animals' personhood and agency, it's also a struggle to readjust the scales of power in favor of the very same individuals from whom power has been withheld.

5

A Vocabulary for Restoring Personhood, Agency, and Power

REALIZING THAT VIOLENCE AGAINST OTHER-THAN-HUMAN ANIMALS manifests itself in insidious ways beyond physical harm was a milestone in the evolution of my thinking. I realized I had hitherto unconsciously condoned or even actively supported not only industries and individuals with the most to gain from exploiting other animals' bodies and labor but also social institutions and norms that rely on and perpetuate the age-old myth that "might makes right," the same supremacist attitude that I, at least in theory, claimed to oppose. Human supremacy takes advantage of other-than-human animals' lack of institutional power to treat them as means to an end, as disposable bodies. Our deliberate invalidation of other animals' individual experiences, our desire to exercise control over every aspect of their lives, *and* our investment in preserving existing uneven power dynamics together uphold a systematic oppression and a faulty ideology, the discursive reproduction of which is a logical, perhaps even inevitable, consequence.

If we now have gender-neutral and gender-diverse titles and pronouns, if derogatory terms such as "faggot" or "retarded" can no longer be thrown around casually (even—or perhaps especially—in comedy, as we collectively recognize that bigotry shouldn't be couched in humor), and if "handicapped" or "disabled" people and "illegal aliens" are now referred to more respectfully as "people with disabilities" and "undocumented immigrants," it's because we recognize that language goes a long way in reshaping the mainstream perception of vulnerable populations. That the language used by the media and popular everyday vernacular both evolved to adopt these intentional shifts in terminology reflects wide-ranging efforts to de-normalize prejudice based on gender or sexuality, physical and mental abilities, or origins.

Today, we still speak of "humane" "meat," "dairy," and "eggs" and "ethically produced" "leather" and "wool"—which are in themselves oxymoronic as these "products" are obtained only through physical and psychological domination. We debate at best dubious policies to imprison other animals in slightly more spacious cages and inject them with fewer antibiotics, but concede that they remain legitimately exploitable. We must destroy the othering that legitimizes this domination and ultimately confront the outdated abstract notion of "the animal" as a monolithic, semi-mystical being standing opposite to us humans. We must view other animals in a different light, and with a different language.

The challenge does not lie just in our ability to feel a certain way toward or to be kind to other-than-human beings. I do not doubt that many of us already feel for at least *some* other animals. Stories of suffering other-than-human individuals tug at our heartstrings, and if we happen to come across such individuals, we often do our best to help them. What is lacking, I believe, is the understanding that other-than-human animals, including those whose suffering we don't see or don't want to see, belong in our moral community. There remains a persistent divide between the few other-than-human animals with whom we get to interact and those who are strangers to us; between the lone resisters whom we occasionally root for—the brave ones who leap from moving transport trucks or fight back against their "trainers" and "carers"—and their peers on the same truck, in the same slaughter chute, or in the same arena.

Studies have shown that the brain structures (including the medial prefrontal cortex) necessary for social cognition—consideration of someone's mind—are activated to lesser degrees in response to social out-groups, namely those that are often perceived as "less than."[1] To lift the barriers to our ability to apply moral rules and values to "outsiders" is to quite literally rewire our brains to be able to see them as individuals whose very beings, mental states, and experiences are loci of value. In doing so, we no longer rely on stereotyping, generalizing, and all other means of distancing and avoiding the "other." Instead, we are forced to consider not only acts of kindness performed to individuals in personal interactions but also our moral responsibility to enact changes that more generally benefit all members of the group.

Charitable organizations and generous individuals everywhere already demonstrate that we understand the moral obligation to help suffering humans on the other side of the globe without having ever met them. That moral behavior that already travels across ethnocultural and geopolitical borders can absolutely defy species divisions, if only we humans critically reexamine the assumption of superiority and self-importance that we have been taught and that we have internalized.

Throughout history, our species has relentlessly sought to display, in whichever way it could, its triumph over nature and all other beings within this domain. To show for it, we have a long, bloodstained record of domesticating and manipulating through selective breeding, capturing and subduing ("taming"), imprisoning, dissecting, probing, and experimenting on other animals only to further reinforce this vague human exceptionalism, to uphold beliefs that we ourselves formed about what it means to be human and about humankind. Other animals have always acted as stand-ins for what we cannot accept: traits and behaviors that might contaminate that idealized vision of ourselves.

To that end, "dehumanization" is said to be the worst form of prejudice. To borrow from feminist philosopher Marilyn Frye, a dominant group's narrowed definition of "human" to encircle only itself is inseparable from a "tendency to romanticize and aggrandize the human species and to derive from one's rosy picture of it a sense of one's individual specialness and superiority." Its appropriation of humanness "is at bottom a version of a self-elevating identification with Humanity."[2] But even when the goal is to eradicate this instrument of oppression, the use of the very word "dehumanization" tacitly centers humanness in ethical discussions and effectively limits the parameters of our moral sphere to include only those of our own species. To recalibrate the conversation to center not humanness but *personhood* and to extend its meaning to other animal species thus constitute the true test of inclusion. In my own work, I've found that the simple act of viewing and *referring to* other-than-human animals as "someone," not "something," already starts to demolish the assumption that a person of rights-worthy moral status is necessarily human.

In 2018, in a historic opinion in response to the Nonhuman Rights Project's petition for the release of Tommy and Kiko, two abused chimpanzees living in captivity, under a writ of *habeas corpus* recognizing their legal personhood and right to bodily liberty, Judge Eugene Fahey of the New York State Court of Appeals concluded: "[W]e should consider whether a chimpanzee is an individual with inherent value who has the right to be treated with respect. . . . While it may be arguable that a chimpanzee is not a 'person,' there is no doubt that it [*sic*] is not merely a thing." Tommy and Kiko, as do all other-than-human animals, have a unique narrative and a unique set of experiences, characteristics, wants, and needs that mark each one's individuality. They are things in neither the legal nor the culturally normative sense.

To deconstruct the homogenous categories into which we've sorted other animals ("test subjects," "entertainers," "food," and so on) in order to recognize each person's individuality necessitates looking past their assigned function or functions. As a 2014 neuroimaging study found, perhaps most unsurprisingly, assigning economic value to individuals results in their "dehumanization," or rather, *depersonification*.[3] To recognize someone's independent worth and personhood is to disregard completely their productive potential—there is no in-between.

Culturally and socially dominant narratives surrounding other-than-human animals often track these prescribed classes of functions in subtle ways. An analysis of the representation of nature on BBC World Service Radio collected fascinating information on the common collocates (words that appear together in the same context) of some other-than-human animal species. The most common collocate of "bird" is "killed"; the most common collocates of "whales" are "killed," "killing," and "hunted." The names of other animals are often accompanied by words indicating human uses for them: for "horse"—"racing"; for "dog"—"trained" and "watch"; for "mice"—"diabetic," "gene," and "liver."[4]

As philosopher Cora Diamond suggests, "[I]t is not because people are capable of reason or language or because they can suffer that we do not eat them. We do not eat them because we do not consider people food. . . . We eat animals because we consider them food."[5] There is a scene in Charlie Chaplin's classic 1925 movie *Gold Rush* in which, stranded together in a blizzard, the starving gold prospector Big Jim sees the Lone Prospector (Chaplin) as a giant chicken and begins to chase him. Even though Chaplin drew inspiration from real-life stories of pioneers who resorted to cannibalism, here the cannibalistic intent is more comedic than unsettling because Chaplin's character is transformed into a "food" animal, thus preserving non-transgressible categories.

Much work will be required to rearrange these hardened mental associations and schemata, yet the underlying conviction is simple: no being exists solely to be cooked up for dinner, endure painful tests for cosmetics, or carry a human around on their back. Being "farmed," being used in laboratories for experiments, and being imprisoned in a marine "park" ("prison" would be an infinitely more apt term) are merely external conditions under which so-called farm or lab animals and the animals at SeaWorld are forced to live, rather than core elements of their identities. They are victims of a violent system, but they are also individuals who exist separately from their place of confinement and the hand of human tyranny.

For allies of other-than-human animals, recognizing them as individuals who exist for their own reasons means that we too need not "cutefy" them or hyperbolize our claims about their cognitive abilities to fit a human mold. It's true that other animals constantly leave us in awe of how well they fare in tests of "human intelligence," but it bears repeating that their mental complexity extends well beyond what they have in common with us, especially when the aim is to elevate their moral status as persons *in spite of* differences in how they experience reality compared to ourselves. Moreover, we have to recognize that misreading is bound to occur when our understanding of other animals is filtered through an imperfect process of interpretation and translation.

It may come as a shock to many that the grinning face chimpanzees make on the covers of Hallmark cards and in TV commercials is actually a "fear grimace" induced by extreme stress. Unsurprisingly, we are inclined to impose on other species associations drawn between certain facial expressions reminiscent of our own and the corresponding internal states in our minds.

As another example, despite many images shared by animal advocates that show other-than-human animals "crying," the jury is still out on whether they actually cry emotional tears. "Humans are pretty fond of giving voices to animals," a 2015 article titled "Do Animals Really Cry?" muses. "Squeaky voices. Excited voices. Princess voices. But do we give them our emotions, too? More specifically, do animals actually cry tears of sorrow?" The author concludes: "Tears are hardly the only way to express pain, but from a human perspective, we rely on them as its most obvious indication." Even if the scientific consensus may be that sad tears are an exclusively human indulgence, does that distinction really matter? "When you harm [other animals], do they not bray and moan and quiver?"[6] Other animals do not need to express emotions exactly as humans do in order for them, and their emotional states, to be credible.

More broadly, I firmly believe that whether or not we can perfectly simulate and capture other animals' subjective experiences in human terms (and I remain doubtful that this is possible or indeed advisable) does not determine their legitimacy as victims of imprisonment, enslavement, sexual violence, or family separation. Acknowledging that these forms of institutionalized violence transcend species boundaries does not diminish human experiences of collective and individual trauma, but it does enhance our understanding of the common strands in narratives of human and other-than-human oppression.

Therein lies the ultimate limitation of the discourse in animal advocacy that uses as its sole leverage point the idea of sameness—that other animals are "just like us"—at the expense of highlighting their own individual dispositions and talents. This discourse reinforces hierarchical logic instead of divorcing from it. It implies that violence against other-than-human animals is objectionable only insofar as they possess a kind of "proxy humanness." Tellingly, a prominent argument for the prosecution of cruel acts toward other-than-human animals is that this cruelty is easily translatable to humans.

As philosopher Kelly Oliver writes, "To insist . . . that our ethical obligations to animals are based on their similarities to us reinforces the type of humanism that leads to treating animals—and other people—as subordinates."[7] Rather, other-than-human beings form a part of our moral community because our interdependence helps us make sense of who we are—because our lives and struggles have always been and continue to be entangled.

Further, to pin our moral decisions on whether we can corroborate or refute an assertion of sameness or difference on a biological basis wrongly assumes that biology is the only criterion for our moral reality. Astoundingly, we have decided we are similar enough to other animals that forcing baby rats to be with abusive foster mothers supposedly offers insights into child abuse in humans; at the same time, we are different enough that *our* "human intelligence" is irreducible to *their* "animal instinct." In a 2015 *Guardian* article that attempted to decode altruism in other-than-human communities, the writer admitted that "[f]orms of altruism are hardwired into all creatures who live in social groups," but then singled out human altruism as unique because, he posited, only humans go out of our way to help complete strangers, whereas "[t]here's no known animal out there who has set up an Oxfam charity so other members of their species could donate."[8]

Since we do not have intimate knowledge of other animals' inner worlds beyond what is educated guesswork based on visual cues, it may very well be that the true motivations behind many behaviors in other animals will forever remain a puzzle. However, to assume that only humans are capable of the kind of noble thought that gives rise to pure altruism, if such entirely selfless actions do exist, is to grossly underestimate our animal kin. Rather than automatically settling for the lazy and convenient explanation that other animals are motivated purely by basic "animal instincts," we have to allow for the possibility that complex layers of intentionality and agency lie beneath their actions.

Other-than-human animals are the owners of their experiences; they are the protagonists of their stories. They are fully capable of speaking for themselves if only given the chance, as Fred the goat and Esther the Wonder Pig have so beautifully demonstrated. When we stop characterizing other animals as "voiceless," we can properly reposition ourselves as their allies. Instead of focusing on a perceived biological defect—that other-than-human individuals are "voiceless," by which we mean they lack *human* voices—thereby exacerbating their otherness, we can start addressing their systematic silencing.

Our commitment to eradicating the "products" of violence currently masquerading as "clothing," "food," "cosmetics," or "entertainment" is a commitment to restoring other animals' ownership of their bodies and labor. Likewise, it is equally our responsibility to return other animals' stories to their rightful owners—to provide a medium through which these stories can be authentically told and to replace noxious cultural stereotypes with undoctored, unexaggerated representations of nonhuman experiences.

We can relay a plain and truthful account of the trauma other animals undergo without reproducing the sterile language industries use in order to normalize their oppressive practices. We do not need to dramatize or sensationalize other-than-human individuals' victimhood, and in so doing subject them once more to the very cultural violence that desensitizes us to their suffering. But if we tell stories about suffering, we ought to also tell stories that highlight courage and resilience—stories that envision a future in which all other-than-human animals may thrive, although this vision is sadly often lost.

In a culture that inculcates and rewards apathy, especially toward those species most commonly exploited for our modern-day conveniences, it sometimes takes descriptions of the most deplorable acts of cruelty to compel the public to consider the other-than-human victims of its choices; such extreme cruelty that borders on sadism often becomes highlighted and foregrounded in animal advocacy discourse. Because some humans still insist on doubting that other animals can indeed suffer, much of this discourse has entailed rebutting the outdated misconception, leaving out crucial questions about what it means for other-than-human animals to not merely exist free from suffering but live fulfilling lives.

If our mission truly is to reaffirm and defend other-than-human animals' personhood and their rights to liberty, sovereignty, and dignity, it is our responsibility to tell, or rather amplify, their individual stories, in which they—the protagonists—take center stage and which honor their individual experiences, personalities, passions, and aspirations. These are not the same story told a billion times over but a billion different stories; they function as reminders that each other-than-human individual's life is as unique and complete as yours or mine and is not reducible to their suffering under human dominance.

*

In the midst of our endless speculation, prodding, and prying, we must recognize other animals as more than blank slates onto which we can project our own devised meanings. Therein lies the difference between true understanding of other animals as they are and mere tolerance, even the kind of tolerance that brands them as those beings who exist "over there," as the "hero," the "underdog," or the "lone resister"—familiar narrative tropes that may instill in us only a superficial sense of pity or admiration. To simply tolerate another is to "hold oneself apart" and erect a "sort of mental barrier" between oneself and the "other."[9] The kind of respectful understanding we ought to seek stems from a will to get closer and to listen. Such an understanding doesn't settle for narratives that are coherent only to us.

But listening to other animals does not come naturally. Because we believe them to be "voiceless," even animal advocates sometimes draw upon the hypothetical conversations that would take place *if* other animals could speak. We lament our inability to (as of yet) truly understand other animals; the assumption is that if *we* could *learn* to communicate with them, their exploitation would cease to be defensible. Although that language barrier is real, premeditated domination of entire species is hardly reducible to simple miscommunication. We don't just lack an understanding of what other animals are saying; we forcibly take away their voices. We refuse to hear them in their native tongues; it's not just that we are not fluent.

Our continual upholding of an anthropocentric definition of "language" (as evidenced by our use of "tongue" as its synonym) obstructs an inter-species and multilingual relationship that often goes beyond what is vocalized: there is more trust conveyed in a cat's slow blink than in many a human's verbal promises. Human language generalizes and categorizes; it abstracts from and occludes reality. Our species takes pride in language as one of its most ingenious creations and one of the most enduring monuments of human civilization, yet it is at best a cloudy medium. Our reality rests on the naïve belief that the stories we tell and the words we have collectively agreed upon are the most accurate representations of the way things truly are, yet these finite words through which we try to capture not only our experiences but the experiences of other animals necessarily fall short of real life.

Even as I attempt to translate what my canine friend, who keeps me company as I write this chapter, is communicating to me into a human language, by means of human vocabulary and expressions, I am putting human words in his mouth—words and meanings already colored by our conceptualization of who he is. As it stands, in order to bring other animals' plights into public consciousness, a lot of the time we necessarily take it upon ourselves to represent their intentions and interests—we speak for them. I am far from condemning what is sometimes the only means for other animals to be heard in a world in which humans' ascendancy over the rest of animalkind seems nearly complete. Nonetheless, our aspirations for better human–other animal communication hinge upon the realization that our understanding is often inadequate, yet our anthropocentric arrogance blinds us to knowledge about other animals that is already there.

With the abundant amount of information now in the public domain, anyone with an Internet connection can see the reality inhabited by the dolled-up elephant who is being stabbed with bullhooks and forced to perform meaningless and pointless tricks in the circus; the maddened lion pacing the length of his cage at the zoo; or the mother cow wailing for her stolen calf on the dairy farm. When we accept as valid and credible what other animals are telling us about their own experiences, it is no longer possible to maintain that these individuals who live under human control not of their own accord are "having fun," that they willingly forego their freedom, or that they are not suffering from psychological distress on top of physical abuse. We can no longer value the marketing claims made by industries above the actual testimonies of their other-than-human victims.

The onus is on us humans to actively seek out narratives different from the ones over which our species has a monopoly and into which we've been socialized. Our understanding may be imperfect and incomplete; however, we must rise to assume the "responsibility to enable responses" from all other beings;[10] we must seek to move in tune with and not impose on them. Knowledge other animals communicate to us about their lives is not a right but a privilege. It is up to us to figure out how to interpret consent from other animals, how to establish respectful communication with them, and how to redefine and co-author our relationships.

☙

We must completely abolish the insidious idea, which is all the more insidious because it is written into the laws and regulations by which we live as well as the language we use in our daily lives, that we can own other animals' bodies and existence. It is absurd to declare ownership of a person with a mind of their own, human or otherwise, even one who may be indebted to us or who is in our care. The idea is as insulting as it is absurd: many of us know that the commitment we make to the other-than-human individuals with whom we choose to share our homes is infinitely more complex than that which binds "owners" to their "pets." For many of us, some of the most profound and long-lasting bonds formed in our lifetimes have been and are with other-than-human companions. When they enter our lives, it is not to be infantilized, paraded around like accessories, dyed various colors, or given funny haircuts.

The other-than-human animals who are kept behind bars and in cages away from our sight, whose basic well-being is disregarded save when it affects the bottom line, are no less autonomous beings with independent worth and no more "property" than those companions of ours. Although legal authorities are almost always on the side of the oppressors, going so far as to charge with burglary the activists who break these horrendously abused individuals out of their prisons, accordance with current laws legitimizes neither their status as *things* to be owned nor their violent exploitation.

Such social structures as the law are in place precisely to protect the status quo. They are designed to withhold institutional power from other-than-human animals and keep them permanently repressed, such that their capacity for self-representation and organized resistance is dismissed as the stuff of fiction (as in the movie *Chicken Run*), and that we continue to see in them beings who are by nature domitable and weak, not a socially marginalized and vulnerable population.

❧

Legally and culturally, the way in which we conceptualize our relationship to other animals still largely limits our corresponding ethical obligation to the prevention of cruelty and mistreatment. Again, I think that our singular focus on *suffering*, as the result of acts of *cruelty*, in the ethical discussion involving other animals tends to overshadow other, equally pressing questions. Importantly, why should it *only* matter when we are *cruel* to them? A lack of outright cruelty does not encompass respect for someone's person. "Cruelty" merely implies an insensitivity to suffering leading to unnecessary or unjustified violence; the exact same outcome may be achieved by means that are "not cruel" or even "humane."

"Humaneness" and "inhumaneness" and, likewise, "humanity" and "inhumanity"—what is human(e) being inherently good and what is inhuman(e) being inherently bad—are notions we continue to borrow wholesale from a millennia-long anthropocentric tradition without much critical (re)examination. As theologian Thomas Aquinas wrote: "Savagery and brutality take their names from a likeness to wild beasts." That the notion of cruelty still carries remnants of its traditional association with beastliness or animality—with the reputed voracity and lack of morality that characterize other-than-human animals—is evidenced in how we respond to displays of cruelty. The punishment for such acts often prescribes a degree of ostracization of the perpetrator as a social deviant, one who is incapable of overcoming their primal "animal" nature.

When an undercover investigation exposes the horrendous violence that is hidden behind the closed doors of a slaughterhouse, we have no trouble condemning the workers who are caught on film, thereby avoiding the need to confront our own complicity. Such a tendency to treat cruelty as a social aberration, as the only morally objectionable aspect of our exploitation of other animals, renders invisible the profoundly human desire to assert dominance for its own sake and to subjugate those who cannot fight back, at the same time as it prevents a truly comprehensive conversation about our ethical obligations to other-than-human beings.

It is high time the animal movement reframed its objectives to aspire to not only negative rights but also positive and affirmative rights for other-than-human animals. Rather than simply specifying what we mustn't do to other animals (thus establishing the foundation for their claim to a negative right), we should also talk about the active steps we ought to take, if within our means and power, to ensure and enhance their quality of life.

The United Nations' Universal Declaration of Human Rights entitles every human being to a "standard of living adequate for the health and well-being of himself and of his family." By contrast, the Five Freedoms, which outline five aspects of animal welfare as formulated by the UK Farm Animal Welfare Council (to use one example of many animal-welfare codes), only protect other-than-human animals living under human control against "unnecessary suffering," such as hunger or thirst, pain, injury or disease, and fear or distress.

Besides the fact that these five provisions are not rights borne by the other-than-human individuals in question and thus are largely ignored in practice, as an article from 2016 points out, the neutralization of these negative experiences in and of itself generates neither good welfare nor a life worth living.[11] A human *rights* violation may not cause actual suffering; it is wrong insofar as it prevents a human from reaching their potential for well-being and happiness. Yet it sometimes takes an appalling degree of physical and mental abuse to elicit outrage from the public and to spur attempted revisions of so-called animal welfare regulations.

Indeed, today the term "animal welfare" has been frequently overused and misused; its meaning has become trite and diluted. Industries' appropriation and distortion of the term, not to mention the repeated failure of welfare legislation to represent the interests of its supposed beneficiaries, have created a rift in how we think about the welfare and the rights of other-than-human animals. The current rights-based movement sometimes removes welfare altogether from its discourse, seeing it as a concept that has become unproductive and ethically dubious. However, we must cease to give validity to this false dichotomy. A sustainable rights framework absolutely needs to encompass a clear understanding of well-being that firmly grounds lofty ideals of dignity, liberty, sovereignty, and justice in practice.

If we are truly prepared to recognize other-than-human animals' experiential subjectivity and capacity for well-being, that means we have to respect not only their basic common interest in not suffering but also each distinct individual's interest in living what they determine to be a good life. We need to consider not only other animals' basic needs, which protect against a diminished quality of life, but also needs that would increase quality of life beyond the subsistence level—idiosyncratic needs for love, hope, healing, and opportunity, which reflect diverse life histories and experiences.

Such considerations already imply an ethic that centers individualized care and ethical responses. In this framework, negative rights would be clearly inadequate in capturing our varying obligations to different individuals in different communities. Indeed, our vision of coexistence and cooperation with other animals would look radically different depending on whether they are free-living animals who have no desire to interact with us, descendants of domesticated animals permanently living under our care, or quasi-dependent animals who have assimilated into human environments and acclimated to our presence. Our ethical obligations to members of each of these groups extend far beyond "leaving them alone," as a well-known motto in animal advocacy goes.

A generalized policy against human interference is arguably no longer feasible in a global ecosphere ravaged by anthropogenic destruction, nor would it be morally unproblematic. Not overtly harming other animals is the bare minimum. An infinitely more nuanced ethical framework may require us to recognize the sovereignty and competence in self-government of free-living populations, and at the same time to empower dependent and quasi-dependent individuals by furnishing them with the tools and skills to navigate the human domain. In recognizing other animals as complex social agents, we neither understate nor overstate our responsibilities. By contrast, in overlooking the nuances of our relationships and the unique needs of each individual, we risk admitting other animals into human society only for them to become second-class citizens subject to a kind of paternalistic protection.

The importance of our affirmative duties as part of an individualized care ethic is made clearest in stories of liberated other-than-human persons. Although their liberation from a life of imprisonment and enslavement (the only life many of them have ever known) is a victory worth celebrating in itself, what is often forgotten is that our work does not end there, and that a long road to rehabilitation and recovery lies ahead. Indeed, not many humans think that other animals can carry or even transmit untreated trauma from physical and psychological abuse to future generations through either genetic mechanisms or socialization. Indeed, we would never think to ask if beings with smaller brains or fewer neurological structures may be *more* susceptible to trauma, since their defenses may be more limited.[12] Those who are in this state of especial vulnerability are most in need of their affirmative rights to protection and resources for recovery.

Further, as members of our moral community, other animals should be able to lay claim to rights that are not only recognized but also upheld by the same rules as are the rights of humans. Human rights are *positive* rights in a second sense—that they oblige active protection: if A has a negative right to life against B, then B is required to refrain from killing A; but if A has a positive right to life against B, then B is required to act to preserve the life of A. We are under obligations, whether legal or moral (or both legal and moral) in character, to honor the rights of our fellow humans. If other-than-human animals' interests are no less legitimate than those of humans and they deserve equal moral consideration, then the same sense of moral duty compels us to guard these interests with equal intensity. If we take our ethical obligations to other animals seriously, we can no longer be complacent bystanders.

⌀

All that being said, the distinctively Western rights-based discourse that is a pillar of the modern animal movement in the West and whose influence is increasingly felt in other cultures is not without its limitations; it shouldn't be immune to critique and revision. It is certainly useful as a commonly understood framework for understanding and formalizing our ethical obligations to our animal kin, not only in the legal and political spheres but also in popular culture. Nonetheless, a rights philosophy inevitably circles back to the exclusionary logic embedded in notions of personhood as well as to political and moral agency as a fundamental rejection of the animal "other" in traditional Western thought. Deeply rooted in Western tradition since Greek antiquity is the dominant definition of an "individualized political subject" who is capable of an independent relationship with the state and thus is in a position to be bestowed rights, namely legal and political rights. Pitted against this inherently anthropocentric image, other-than-human animals inevitably come up short; they appear "less than" and powerless.[13]

As philosopher Kelly Oliver eloquently reasons, "Even if moving people or animals from one side of the man–animal divide to the other may change our attitudes toward them, it does not necessarily transform the oppositional logic that pits *us* versus *them* and justifies our enslaving, imprisoning, or torturing (not to mention eating) *them*." French philosopher Jacques Derrida even goes so far as to express skepticism toward the very concept of rights as they apply to other-than-human animals, deeming it a product of an inherently speciesist tradition: "To confer or to recognize rights for 'animals' is a surreptitious or implicit way of confirming a certain interpretation of the human subject, which itself will have been the very lever of the worst violence carried out against nonhuman living beings."[14]

Heeding both thinkers' warnings, we must not uncritically accept the Western conceptualization of rights and its accompanying logic; we must not merely reposition the dividing line to allow other animals (or merely certain groups of "higher" animals, which the fight for legal nonhuman personhood currently spotlights) to join us in the category of "human." Instead, we must transform our gaze upon other animals and invite them to vindicate themselves in their own right. Our challenge is not to see other-than-human persons as wearers of human masks, but rather to engage with them in all their other-than-humanness.

For this very reason, I believe the idea of "animal rights" is even more radical than it may seem at first glance. It entails not merely extending what are now considered fundamental *human* rights to other animals; it defies the entirety of the Western canon by asking us to question that what we call rights are rooted in the human experience to begin with.

Rights originated from a dominant group's desire to elevate its own interests above those of not only other-than-human animals but also all the other humans whom that group decided operated outside the realm of moral concern. Rights were initially reserved only for members of that in-group, while those outside of this narrow sphere were conferred zero rights. Little by little, and at great cost, out-group humans (communities of different races, geopolitical origins, genders, sexual orientations, and neurological makeups) have forced the extension of some of the rights monopolized by the elite in-group. Usually, the dominant group only tolerates progress and foregoes some of its status so long as that progress creates little competition for the privileges it is accustomed to enjoying and so long as it is sufficiently reassured that the social hierarchy will not be threatened or unraveled.

In spite of this deeply ingrained and problematic way of thinking, human atrocities have sometimes led to rare moments of common clarity for our species. In the aftermath of World War II, the drafting and adoption of the Universal Declaration of Human Rights offered a step, however small, toward the collective understanding that there was, and remains, a set of inalienable, pre-legal rights that should be enjoyed by every human, although the debate as to which exact rights are "universal" and should be included is ongoing.

I believe there are grounds for optimism. Whereas its history is stacked against other animals, a philosophy of human rights may be rewritten and reclaimed as the backbone of our vision of a future world defined by equitable inter-species coexistence. In this world, what our predecessors have written on notions like sovereignty, liberty, and integrity of one's person serve as valuable standards for how we treat different communities of other-than-human individuals. As we continue to explore the manifold ethical obligations we already owe other animals but have not hitherto honored, let us remember that the concept of "rights" is after all a tool for enforcing our moral duties to one another. If we're constantly challenging the false boundaries of our imaginary circle of individuals worthy of moral status, perhaps there may even come a time when we finally realize that we never needed to define one in the first place—that our identity need not be defined in opposition to another's identity and that our well-being need not be achieved at the expense of another's.

6

Final Words

T HERE IS LITTLE DOUBT IN MY MIND THAT UNIVERSAL LIBERTY and justice for other-than-human animals are not only possible but imminent. To acknowledge other animals' claims to fundamental rights and protections is to unlink from the narrative of human superiority that we have told and retold time and again. To recognize our shared animality and moral worth is to confront and demolish an age-old species hierarchy that has been naturalized and engraved in all human social institutions. Doing so is thus seen as a step backward and a violation of the very order of the natural world rather than the overcoming of a harmful social construction.

But let us remember that "the animal" is not so much a natural as a sociopolitical and metaphorical being, who has inspired great inconsistencies and ambivalence rather than moral consensus among different religious and philosophical traditions throughout history; new scientific understanding then, as now, only further complicated the "question of the animal" rather than demystifying it. Specifically, the strict human–animal dualism that we have inherited today and that has been propagated beyond the West was a deliberate invention born of Cartesian philosophy and the scientific revolution. In recognizing that our absolute superiority to other animals is a figment of our imagination and that the values we assign to other animals are arbitrary, not handed to us by some external, divine force, we begin to dismantle the fallacies that uphold human supremacy.

It bears repeating that our work to reestablish and reaffirm other animals' personhood, agency, and exercise of power—to recognize their rights to be regarded and treated with dignity—is not limited to the act of replacing certain words and phrases. We need to challenge speciesist discourse at its core. Our goal is not to "veganize" our vernacular as we do a recipe or our wardrobes—simply replacing foodstuffs and products in our daily lives without being critical of our broken production system and envisioning its reinvention and innovation. Instead, we ought to rewrite our collective history so as to recognize not only the place other animals have always had in our lives but also their inherent dignity as beings who don't owe their existence to a human creator, benefactor, or savior.

An accurate retelling of that shared history would hinge upon the humble recognition that in other animals we find wisdom imbued with a purposefulness and honesty that our education and cultural conditioning have driven us to abandon. Long ago, other animals functioned as teachers to our ancestors, who not only observed and mimicked them from a distance but also tried to embody this wisdom, which stood in stark contrast to the "brutal" (in the literal sense of the word), mechanistic animality and material reality we claim to have transcended.[1] This is not to make the common mistake that we can look with rose-tinted glasses on a more perfect point in our past that supposedly holds the answers to all of our ethical dilemmas. To truly integrate other-than-human persons into human society is something humankind has never quite successfully done or maybe even attempted. However, the moral imperative to do so is stronger now than ever.

Considering that so many groups of humans have throughout history been marginalized through an association with other-than-human animals, there is, understandably, a strong desire to resist and dismiss an analysis of oppression that addresses this same "question of the animal." However, the more we disconnect from or exclude other animals from our vision of moral progress, the more we reinforce the dichotomous paradigm of "us" versus "them" that threatens to make any gains in terms of social equity temporary and fragile. When there are terms and conditions that delimit our pursuit of justice, these terms can easily be revoked. When the secureness of the oppressors' power depends on this fragmentation of narratives of oppression, entire communities are pitted against each other. They are fed a false narrative of scarcity and fooled into negotiating their rights like a zero-sum game, forgetting that rights are not a finite resource and are withheld from them only by the powers that be. To purposely choose to recognize the moral standing of other-than-human animals, whose silencing and disenfranchisement are very nearly complete, is a radical act of resistance.

Often, the struggle for nonhuman liberation is misrepresented as a toss-up between the rights of humans and the rights of other animals. In our anthropocentric arrogance, we hurriedly resolve that perceived conflict by declaring that only human rights are non-negotiable. Many people, including vegans, would agree without hesitation that the right of a single human trumps that of many other-than-human individuals. "If you could save one human child, how many animals would you be willing to sacrifice?" is the kind of question we ponder. A quick look at current practices in vivisection, animal agribusiness, and captivity reveals the answer: hundreds, even thousands, to one.

In reality, progress toward the liberation of one group likely also benefits others. The abolition of a production system whose *modus operandi* is to manipulate the bodily autonomy and life cycles of other-than-human beings for profit would also benefit the slaughterhouse workers who suffer from PTSD, the rural communities ravaged by air and water pollution produced by CAFOs, and the black and brown youth targeted by fast-food commercials who are set on a path to lifelong chronic illnesses. Even when our interests and the interests of other animals do diverge, the ethical gravity of such conflicts of interest warrants serious deliberation. Provided we constantly reassess and renegotiate our ethical obligations to other animals, the nuances of each conflict that arises would be far too numerous to permit a one-size-fits-all response.

In the same vein, the outrage and sense of injustice we feel whenever a human is said to be "treated like an animal" present opportunities to combat the underlying vulnerability experienced by both human *and* other-than-human beings and to validate the moral status of both. To overturn the human supremacist ideology that exempts us from having to consider our animal kin and reclaim the word "animal" is to simultaneously neutralize the kind of "animalizing" discourse that is used to demean and subjugate our fellow humans.

The urgency of both tasks is palpable, especially considering that we are witnessing in today's political landscape the convergence of multiple axes of oppression at their most violent extremes, such that the important links between them are difficult to miss. We must stop overlooking the ways in which other animals figure into the propagation of structural violence and into our understanding of racialized, gendered, age- or class-based, and other forms of human conflict. The time for this conversation is *now*.

The animal rights discourse we need and should aspire to is one that unmistakably states our uncompromised vision of justice and equity for other animals in a language that is accessible but equally uncompromising. Although it is uncomfortable to acknowledge that one's everyday vernacular, as is the case with purchasing choices, may not reflect one's values, language remains an important component of moral and social progress. Every day, we are given many opportunities to act in alignment with our ethical obligations to other animals, and we have the ability to choose our words carefully to reflect the same moral duties. Speciesist discourse must be challenged in private and in public, in informal and formal settings, in writing and in conversations.

In our efforts to build a personal and collective anti-speciesist vocabulary, we may find that some parts of language are more resistant to change than others depending on how our brains process them. Nouns, verbs, and adjectives—so-called open-class words—are open to addition, subtraction, and revision, not unlike software. Words that describe novel inventions and concepts, such as "vegan," were coined and gained relatively quick acceptance. "Closed class" words, including pronouns, are more like hardware; we use them so often and so unconsciously that restructuring them is much trickier.

Then there are also difficulties and limitations that are specific to each language. The Vietnamese language, for example, replicates the cultural preoccupation with maintaining the social order through the rich syntax and vocabulary one uses to address and refer to another person. Factors that affect the syntax and vocabulary chosen include one's age relative to the other person, one's relationship with that person, one's social status, and so on. As such, an alternative to this characteristically anthropocentric linguistic system isn't obvious, and I do not claim to have it all figured out. To redefine and replace the boundaries of linguistic conventions that are grounded in anthropocentrism—that are intended to be applicable only to human relationships—will undoubtedly require not only conviction but also a lot of creativity.

That hard-to-break linguistic habits can serve to cement morally outdated ideas raises the very real question of how to engage with another person who operates within a vastly different vocabulary and, by extension, on a different ideological plane. I have experienced great frustration talking to an old friend (whom I love dearly) who did not see an issue with the non-literal use of "retarded," a word I had long banished. The same communication lapse arises when I try to bring attention to speciesist language. I have at times found myself almost "speaking a different tongue" and having to engage with people who don't understand, appreciate, or necessarily want to use the terms that I do. I admittedly raise some eyebrows every now and again when I speak of other animals as persons, or when, in my native Vietnamese, I refer to them using the plural pronoun usually reserved for only humans (*họ*), rather than the dismissive *chúng* or *chúng nó*. And, admittedly, when writing in Vietnamese, I sometimes still find myself avoiding the use of pronouns altogether lest the reader is thrown off by the sight and sound of an unconventional pronoun.

Unsurprisingly, since speciesism is a consistent phenomenon across human cultures, it is also deeply embedded in more languages than one. Indeed, the precise institutionalized practices of nonhuman exploitation may be specific to a culture or an economy; some of us may have grown up eschewing "meat" and other "animal products" for cultural or religious reasons, or never knowing circuses and zoos as children. However, we were all raised human, including those of us who later turned our backs on the speciesist ideology; we all learned from the moment we were born that humans can do with other animals whatever we please. Not a few activists no doubt have come to the deeply disturbing realization that they could so easily act out an oppressive script and flaunt their power as oppressors; they could much more easily and with impunity choose indifference and even malice over understanding and respect.

Despite our most conscientious efforts to unlearn a speciesist mother tongue, out of habit words like "pets" sometimes find their way back to our lips. To attempt to undo all of the cultural conditioning to which we have been exposed for years—in order to alter not only how we live our lives but how we communicate—is an ambitious endeavor. We are almost certain to not get it perfectly right on the first try; but try we must.

Anyone who has had to navigate more than one culture in their lifetime can perhaps appreciate that our efforts to tackle discursive speciesism will look different in different sociopolitical and cultural contexts depending on, for example, how rigidly discursive norms are safeguarded and how acceptable alternative cultural narratives are perceived to be. Another important consideration is that the available conceptual repertoire and vocabulary for expressing abstract notions such as personal liberty and rights or simply for describing subjective mental states differ greatly between collectivistic cultures and individualistic ones, in which the "I" reigns supreme.

But whatever the linguistic domain or whatever the cultural context we operate in, we cannot eradicate speciesism if we continue to tolerate it in the very words we speak. We cannot rethink our relationships with other animals if we as their self-appointed allies do not fundamentally reshape our language and narratives so as to speak from a place of understanding and acknowledgment of their individual persons.

I hope that we continue to take courage—that instead of "taking the bull by the horns," we metaphorically "take the flower by the thorns"—to confront linguistic traditions that perpetuate violence and injustice, because more than semantics is at stake. It's only by doing so that we'll finally be able to give other animals the respect we've owed them since the very beginning.

7

The Other-Than-Human People Who Teach Us Humanity

IDEDICATE THESE LAST PAGES TO A SERIES OF PORTRAITS OF OTHER-than-human animals. To me, portraiture in its most faithful expression is a means of conveying a piece of an individual as they are, mired in neither the imposed demands of others nor the pressure to fit into a predetermined narrative.

Not every portrait is accompanied by details about the subject's life, and that is intentional. In reality, the level of interaction we share with many other-than-human individuals is usually limited to brief chance encounters, the duration of which do not afford us the luxury of discovering their stories. The chances are that many of these individuals will go through their entire lives without ever being fully known by a human.

Collectively, we humans boast an abundant repertoire of stories about other animals' lives. Some of these are fairytales and stories of hope and healing. Others are downright heartbreaking, with not a glimpse of human kindness. Some of these other-than-human individuals, by virtue of the symbolic power of their species or their tragic backstories, live a portion of their lives in the limelight; their names are inscribed on petitions and the public consciousness for years to come. Others—most other-than-human persons—die in anonymity, having at best been identified by a serial number.

In any case, what we know of their stories is beside the point. Each person's story is known to them, if no one else. It is a rather unsettling realization: that human perception and understanding are not required for an other-than-human person to exist and persist or for their subjective experience to be extraordinary—that without any need to be seen and known by a human or validated by human constructions of reality, other-than-human animals continue to live with meaning and purpose.

Even so, these portraits of other animals need to be made visible to humans because as advocates standing in solidarity with them (as I am fully aware my role is in writing this book) we are putting ourselves in conversation with humankind, which, as of now, alone wields the choice of organizing, advocating, and legislating either to continue enslaving other-than-human persons as we have always done or to usher in a paradigm shift. Because we have rendered other animals "absent referents" (a term utilized most powerfully by Carol J. Adams)—flesh-and-blood beings who disappear in the course of the commodification of their bodies—to be able to truly see them is a significant feat.

To truly see other animals is to simultaneously come to terms with our own vulnerability and to accept difference as a fact of life, thus rejecting the idea that only those who remind us of ourselves can demand respect. "Respect" comes from the Latin *respectus*, literally meaning "to look back," "to look again." It is thus through painting new portraits of other animals, literally and figuratively, that we are bid to look and acknowledge them in their inherent dignity. That we are finally entering an era in which that dignity is seen and remembered is a sight to behold.

In memoriam: Blake
She was a true matriarch.
(Reproduced with permission from VINE Sanctuary, from a photograph by Selena Salfen)

Honey
Who was so generous with her trust, for whom we could do so little.

In memoriam: Stevia
Though she could never return to her true home, she showed her human companions her true adventurous self.
(Reproduced with permission from Rachel Lee Cascada)

Pearl
She faced the unknown in quiet calmness and dignity.

Bubbles
Her playfulness delights as much as her unapologetic presence inspires.

Floyd
His disability never stopped him from living life to the fullest.

In memoriam: Win Title
She was so much more than her ability to win.

In memoriam: Olive
She was loved until the end.

In memoriam: Roux
His brilliant blue hue was not meant to be, nor did it define him.
(Reproduced with permission from Rachel Lee Cascada)

In memoriam
Someone I would have liked to have known, who bore the unbearable.

Acknowledgments

UNTIL A YEAR AND A HALF AGO, I HAD NEVER GIVEN MUCH THOUGHT to the prospect of writing a book. This book came into existence rather serendipitously and wholly thanks to those whose guidance I am beyond lucky to have received. To Ingrid Newkirk, Philip Schein, and Ryan Huling: thank you for helping me define my place in the animal movement, for inspiring the conception of this book, and for your feedback and constant encouragement from the first rough outline to the last edits.

I thank my family members, especially my mother, whose support fuels my confidence in my chosen path of advocacy. More important, I thank them for being an endless source of material for personal anecdotes for this book. Writing it would not have been nearly as enjoyable without their appearances.

Special thanks go to my editor, Martin Rowe, for his patience and the immense support he was willing to offer a first-time author, even as my perfectionism and nervousness about publication no doubt made for an arduous process.

Last but not least, I'd like to express my deepest gratitude to everyone, human and otherwise, whom I have the fortune to know or have conversed with, whose insights, personal stories, or simple presence inspired me greatly. Among them are college students across North America whom I met during my travels, activists, and scholars, whose vision, wealth of knowledge, and dedication to the liberation of other-than-human beings continue to inform my own views. This lengthy list also includes the many other-than-human people who never cease to amaze me with their mischief, love, and resilience; some of them were kind enough to keep me company during my hours of writing and editing the manuscript. To these people: I owe the thoughts and ideas that have become this book in large part to all of you.

Selected Bibliography

Adams, Carol J. *The Sexual Politics of Meat: A Feminist-Vegetarian Critical Theory*. 20th Anniversary ed. New York: Continuum International Publishing Group, 2009.

Adams, Carol J., and Josephine Donovan. *Animals and Women: Feminist Theoretical Explorations*. Durham, NC: Duke University Press, 1995.

Borkfelt, Sune. "What's in a Name?—Consequences of Naming Non-Human Animals." *Animals* 1, no. 1 (March 2011): 116–25.

Derrida, Jacques. *The Animal That Therefore I Am*. Edited by Marie-Louise Mallet. Translated by David Wills. New York: Fordham University Press, 2008.

Donaldson, Brianne. "Discourse First, Cages Second: A New Locus for Animal Liberation." *Between the Species* 10 (August 2010): 204–22.

Donaldson, Sue, and Will Kymlicka. *Zoopolis: A Political Theory of Animal Rights*. Oxford, UK: Oxford University Press, 2011.

Dunayer, Joan. *Animal Equality: Language and Liberation*. Derwood, MD: Ryce Publishing, 2001.

Gruen, Lori. *Entangled Empathy: An Alternative Ethic for Our Relationships with Animals*. New York: Lantern Books, 2014.

Jepson, Jill. "A Linguistic Analysis of Discourse on the Killing of Nonhuman Animals." *Society & Animals* 16 (2008): 127–48.

Ko, Aph, and Syl Ko. *Aphro-ism: Essays on Pop Culture, Feminism, and Black Veganism from Two Sisters*. New York: Lantern Books, 2017.

Oliver, Kelly. *Animal Lessons: How They Teach Us to Be Human*. New York: Columbia University Press, 2009.

Paterson, David, and Richard D. Ryder, eds. *Animals' Rights — a Symposium*. New York: Centaur Press, 1979.

Regan, Tom. *The Case for Animal Rights*. 2nd ed. Berkeley: University of California Press, 2004.

Regan, Tom, and Peter Singer, eds. *Animal Rights and Human Obligations*. 2nd ed. Upper Saddle River, NJ: Prentice Hall, 1989.

Singer, Peter. *Animal Liberation*. 4th ed. New York: HarperCollins, 2009.

Spiegel, Marjorie. *The Dreaded Comparison: Human and Animal Slavery*. London: Heretic, 1988.

Stibbe, Arran. "Language, Power and the Social Construction of Animals." *Society & Animals* 9, no. 2 (2001): 145–61.

Taylor, Sunaura. *Beasts of Burden: Animal and Disability Liberation*. New York: The New Press, 2017.

Notes

1: Other Animals, According to Humans: A Very Brief History

1. It should be noted that "Western" and "Eastern" are geopolitical designations that grow out of, and to an extent depend on, a colonialized relationship. The "West" has long demarcated itself as rational, monotheistic, and enlightened in comparison with the "East," a vast and diverse geographic region that encompasses all of Asia and upon which the "West" has imposed orientalist notions of sensuality, polytheism, and superstition. As someone in both worlds, I reject these binaries, even while acknowledging that they serve as a useful shorthand to differentiate different philosophical etiologies and worldviews.

2. Tom Hawkins, "Eloquent Alogia: Animal Narrators in Ancient Greek Literature," *Humanities* 6, no. 2 (June 2017): 37.

3. Thorsten Fögen, "Lives in Interaction: Animal 'Biographies' in Graeco-Roman Literature?", in *Interactions Between Animals and Humans in Graeco-Roman Antiquity*, eds. Thorsten Fögen and Edmund Thomas (Berlin: De Gruyter, 2017), 89–138.

4. Johanna Leah Braff, "Animal Similes and Gender in the *Odyssey* and *Oresteia*" (Master's thesis, University of Maryland, 2008).

5. Steven D. Smith, "Monstrous Love? Erotic Reciprocity in Aelian's *De natura animalium*," in *Erôs in Ancient Greece*, eds. Ed Sanders, Chiara Thumiger, Christopher Carey, and N. J. Lowe (Oxford, UK: Oxford University Press, 2013), 73–89.

6. Laurie Shannon, "The Eight Animals in Shakespeare; or, Before the Human," *PMLA* 124, no. 2 (March 2009): 472–9.

7. Tom MacFaul, "Shakespeare's Animals," filmed in 2015 at University of Oxford, Oxford, United Kingdom, video at: www.youtube.com/watch?v=Xn71LnPmyQM.

8. Thomas Henry Huxley, *Evidence as to Man's Place in Nature* (London: Williams & Norgate, 1863).

9. Ruiping Fan, "How Should We Treat Animals? A Confucian Reflection," *Dao* 9, no. 1 (2010): 79–96.

10. Joseph A. Adler, "Response to Rodney Taylor, 'Of Animals and Man: The Confucian Perspective,'" presented at Conference on Religion and Animals, Harvard-Yenching Institute, Cambridge, Mass., 1999.

11. E. N. Anderson and Lisa Raphals, "Daoism and Animals," in *A Communion of Subjects: Animals in Religion, Science & Ethics*, eds. Paul Waldau and Kimberley C. Patton (New York: Columbia University Press, 2006), 278.

12. Lisa Kemmerer, "The Great Unity: Daoism, Nonhuman Animals, and Human Ethics," *Journal for Critical Animal Studies* 7, no. 2 (2009): 63–83.

13. Emmeline Cambridge, *Exploring the Effect of Imagery and Categorisation on Belief in Animal Mind* (Hamburg, Germany: Anchor Academic Publishing, 2015), 22.

14. Dominique Patton, "China's Multi-Story Hog Hotels Elevate Industrial Farms to New Levels," *Reuters*, May 10, 2018.

2: "It's Just an Animal": How Language Takes Away Personhood

1. "Probe: Ex-Officer Called Black Teen 'Wild Animal' in Post," *Associated Press*, July 23, 2018.

2. Hope Ferdowsian, *Phoenix Zones: Where Strength Is Born and Resilience Lives* (Chicago, Ill.: University of Chicago Press, 2018), 3.

3. Kien Nguyen, "Daily Deference Rituals and Social Hierarchy in Vietnam," *Asian Social Science* 12, no. 5 (2016): 33–46.

4. Otto Jespersen, *A Modern English Grammar: On Historical Principles, Part II: Syntax* (First Volume) (London: Bradford & Dickens, 1954).

5. Tom Regan, *The Case for Animal Rights*, 2nd ed. (Berkeley: University of California Press, 2004), xvi.

6. Lindsay Boyle, "Motor Malfunction Believed to Have Caused Lebanon Fire that Killed at Least 80,000 Chickens," *The Day*, April 27, 2016.

7.   Christina Succi, "Quinte West Barn Fire Leaves 1200 Pigs Dead," *CTV Ottawa*, December 11, 2018.

8.   Ronald H. Bayor, ed., *The Oxford Handbook of American Immigration and Ethnicity* (Oxford, UK: Oxford University Press, 2016).

9.   Christina M. Colvin and Lori Marino, "Signs of Intelligent Life: Pigs Possess Complex Ethological Traits Similar to Dogs and Chimpanzees," *Natural History*, October 2015.

10. Lori Marino, "Thinking Chickens: A Review of Cognition, Emotion, and Behavior in the Domestic Chicken," *Animal Cognition* 20, no. 2 (2017): 127–47.

11. Inbal Ben-Ami Bartal, Jean Decety, and Peggy Mason, "Empathy and Pro-Social Behavior in Rats," *Science* 334, no. 6061 (2011): 1427–30.

12. Roger Fouts and Stephen Tukel Mills, *Next of Kin: My Conversations with Chimpanzees* (New York: William Morrow, 1997).

13. Caroline Davies, "How Do Homing Pigeons Navigate? They Follow Roads," *Telegraph* (UK), February 5, 2004.

14. Anil Seth, "Your Brain Hallucinates Your Conscious Reality," filmed April 2017 at TED2017, video at: https://www.ted.com/talks/anil_seth_how_your_brain_hallucinates_your_conscious_reality.

15. Mihnea Tanasescu, "When a River Is a Person: From Ecuador to New Zealand, Nature Gets Its Day in Court," *The Conversation*, June 19, 2017.

3: "Animal Instinct": How Language Takes Away Agency

1.   Benjamin Reiss, "Why Do We Make Children Sleep Alone?" *Los Angeles Times*, March 24, 2017.

2.   Dave Rogers, "Strange Noises Turn Out to Be Cows Missing Their Calves," *Daily News of Newburyport*, October 23, 2013.

3.   Sandhya Somashekhar and Amy B. Wang, "Lawmaker Who Called Pregnant Women a 'Host' Pushes Bill Requiring Fathers to Approve Abortion," *Washington Post*, February 14, 2017.

4.   Theresa Corrigan and Stephanie Hoppe, eds., *And a Deer's Ear, Eagle's Song and Bear's Grace: Animals and Women* (Pittsburgh, Penn.: Cleis Press, 1990), 199–200.

5.   "The Ultimate Sacrifice: Mother Bear Kills Her Cub and Then Herself to Save Her from a Life of Torture," *Daily Mail*, August 12, 2011.

6.   Candice Gaukel Andrews, "Is Animal Altruism Real?" *Good Nature Travel*, February 5, 2013.

7.   Tom Polansek and P. J. Huffstutter, "As Hurricane Nears, U.S. Farmers Rush to Clear Crops but Animals Stay in Storm's Path," *Reuters*, September 11, 2018.

8.   For more on the origins of our domestication of other-than-human animals, see Jim Mason's *An Unnatural Order: The Roots of Our Destruction of Nature* (New York: Lantern Books, 2005).

9.   Adam S. Wilkins, Richard W. Wrangham, and W. Tecumseh Fitch, "The 'Domestication Syndrome' in Mammals: A Unified Explanation Based on Neural Crest Cell Behavior and Genetics," *Genetics* 197, no. 3 (2014): 795–808.

10.   Carrie Murphy, "The Husband Stitch Isn't Just a Horrifying Childbirth Myth," *Healthline*, January 24, 2018.

11.   Sunaura Taylor, *Beasts of Burden: Animal and Disability Liberation* (New York: The New Press, 2017).

12.   Karen Davis, "The Provocative Elitism of 'Personhood' for Nonhuman Creatures in Animal Advocacy Parlance and Polemics," *Journal of Evolution and Technology* 24, no. 3 (2014): 35–43.

13.   "Rescued Piglets Served Up as Sausages to Firefighters," *BBC News*, August 23, 2017.

14.   Keith Thomas, *Man and the Natural World: Changing Attitudes in England 1500–1800* (London: Penguin Books, 1984), 20.

4: "Like an Animal": How Language Takes Away Power

1.   Kate Bernot, "Esther the Wonder Pig Denied Chemo Treatment Because She Is 'Food,'" *The Takeout*, September 7, 2018.

2.   Arran Stibbe, "Language, Power and the Social Construction of Animals," *Society and Animals* 9, no. 2 (2001): 145–61.

3.   Malachi Barrett, "Coldwater Pork Company Says Hog Transporters Risked Animal Safety in Cold Weather," *MLive*, January 31, 2019.

4.   Steven LeVine, "Facial Recognition Is Extended to Pigs," *Axios*, June 13, 2018.

5.   Hilary Hanson, "Escaped Goat, Rumored to Have Freed Others from Slaughter, Has Been Captured," *Huffington Post*, August 30, 2018.

6. Sune Borkfelt, "Non-Human Otherness: Animals as Others and Devices for Othering," in *Otherness: A Multilateral Perspective*, eds. Susan Yi Sencindiver, Maria Beville, and Marie Lauritzen (Frankfurt am Main, Germany: Peter Lang, 2011), 137–54.

7. Maria Dolan, "The Gruesome History of Eating Corpses as Medicine," *Smithsonian Magazine*, May 6, 2012.

8. "Kansas City Zoo Fixing Exhibit After Orangutan's Climb," *Associated Press*, July 5, 2016.

9. Melanie Joy, *Why We Love Dogs, Eat Pigs, and Wear Cows: An Introduction to Carnism* (Newburyport, Mass.: Conari Press, 2009), 29–30.

10. Ben Graham and Natalie Wolfe, "PETA Sparks Outrage by Barbecuing 'Dog' in Mall," *New York Post*, January 24, 2019.

11. Jessica Durando, "Donald Trump Jr. Compares Border Wall to Zoo Fences that Hold Animals in Instagram Post," *USA Today*, January 9, 2019.

12. Frederick Merk, *Manifest Destiny and Mission in American History: A Reinterpretation* (Cambridge, Mass.: Harvard University Press, 1963), 3.

13. Quoted in Keith Thomas, *Man and the Natural World: Changing Attitudes in England 1500–1800* (London: Penguin Books, 1984), 21.

14. Sune Borkfelt, "What's in a Name?—Consequences of Naming Non-Human Animals," *Animals* 1, no. 1 (March 2011): 116–25.

15. S. J. Gould, "Morton's Ranking of Races by Cranial Capacity: Unconscious Manipulation of Data May Be a Scientific Norm," *Science* 200, no. 4341 (1978): 503–9.

16. Londa Schiebinger, "Why Mammals Are Called Mammals: Gender Politics in Eighteenth-Century Natural History," *American Historical Review* 98, no. 2 (1993): 382–411.

17. Marjorie Spiegel, *The Dreaded Comparison: Human and Animal Slavery* (London: Heretic, 1988), 25.

18. Wulf D. Hund and Charles W. Mills, "Comparing Black People to Monkeys Has a Long, Dark Simian History," *The Conversation*, February 28, 2016.

19. Daniel Pollack-Pelzner, "'Mary Poppins,' and a Nanny's Shameful Flirting with Blackface," *New York Times*, January 28, 2019.

20. Quoted in Sunaura Taylor, *Beasts of Burden: Animal and Disability Liberation* (New York: The New Press, 2017).

21. Anya Stanley, "Not Your Trophy: Deer Imagery in Jordan Peele's 'Get Out,'" *Vague Visages*, March 22, 2017.

22. Paul Bloom, "The Root of All Cruelty?", *The New Yorker*, November 27, 2017.

23. Marilynn B. Brewer, "The Psychology of Prejudice: Ingroup Love or Outgroup Hate?" *Journal of Social Issues* 55, no. 3 (1999): 429–44.

5: A Vocabulary for Restoring Personhood, Agency, and Power

1. Lasana T. Harris and Susan T. Fiske, "Dehumanizing Perception: A Psychological Means to Facilitate Atrocities, Torture, and Genocide?", *Z Psychology* 219, no. 3 (2011): 175–81.

2. Quoted in Joan Dunayer, "Sexist Words, Speciesist Roots," *in Animals and Women: Feminist Theoretical Explorations*, eds. Carol J. Adams and Josephine Donovan (Durham, NC: Duke University Press, 1995), 11–27.

3. L. T. Harris, V. K. Lee, B. H. Capestany, and A. O. Cohen, "Assigning Economic Value to People Results in Dehumanization Brain Response," *Journal of Neuroscience, Psychology, and Economics* 7, no. 3 (2014), 151–63.

4. Jill Jepson, "A Linguistic Analysis of Discourse on the Killing of Nonhuman Animals," *Society and Animals* 16 (2008): 127–48.

5. Kelly Oliver, "Animal Ethics: Toward an Ethics of Responsiveness," *Research in Phenomenology* 40 (2010): 267–80.

6. Christian Cotroneo, "Do Animals Really Cry?", *The Dodo*, November 3, 2015.

7. Kelly Oliver, "Animal Ethics: Toward an Ethics of Responsiveness," *Research in Phenomenology* 40 (2010): 267–80.

8. David Cox, "Rationing Ravens and Merciful Monkeys: Can Animals Be Altruistic?" *Guardian*, January 26, 2015.

9. Quoted in Theresa Corrigan and Stephanie Hoppe, eds., *And a Deer's Ear, Eagle's Song and Bear's Grace: Animals and Women* (Pittsburgh, Penn.: Cleis Press, 1990), 215.

10. Kelly Oliver, "Animal Ethics: Toward an Ethics of Responsiveness," *Research in Phenomenology* 40 (2010): 267–80.

11. David J. Mellor, "Updating Animal Welfare Thinking: Moving Beyond the 'Five Freedoms' Towards 'A Life Worth Living,'" *Animals* 6, no. 3 (2016): 21.

12. Hope Ferdowsian, *Phoenix Zones: Where Strength Is Born and Resilience Lives* (Chicago, Ill.: University of Chicago Press, 2018), 37.

13. Brianne Donaldson, "Discourse First, Cages Second: A New Locus for Animal Liberation," *Between the Species* 10 (August 2010): 204–22.

14. Kelly Oliver, "Animal Ethics: Toward an Ethics of Responsiveness," *Research in Phenomenology* 40 (2010): 267–80.

6: Final Words

1. Brianne Donaldson, "Discourse First, Cages Second: A New Locus for Animal Liberation," *Between the Species* 10 (August 2010): 204–22.

About the Author

HANH NGUYEN holds a BA in Sociology from Yale University. Her journey in rethinking human–other animal relationships began when she was an undergraduate, and has since taken her to dozens of colleges and universities across North America, helping thousands of students examine their own perceptions of other-than-human animals.

About the Publisher

LANTERN BOOKS was founded in 1999 on the principle of living with a greater depth and commitment to the preservation of the natural world. In addition to publishing books on animal advocacy, vegetarianism, religion, and environmentalism, Lantern is dedicated to printing books in the U.S. on recycled paper and saving resources in day-to-day operations. Lantern is honored to be a recipient of the highest standard in environmentally responsible publishing from the Green Press Initiative.

LANTERNBOOKS.COM